GOING FOR BROKER

Derek Tullett: A life in the City and beyond

With best wishes
Derek Tullett Sepr 2007

GOING FOR BROKER

Derek Tullett
A life in the City and beyond

Matador
9 De Montfort Mews
Leicester LE1 7FW, UK
Tel: (+44) 116 255 9311 / 9312
Email: books@troubador.co.uk
Web: www.troubador.co.uk/matador

ISBN: 978-1905886-944

Print Management by Image Production Ltd London.

Typeset in 12.5pt Garamond by Troubador Publishing Ltd, Leicester, UK
Printed in the UK by The Cromwell Press Ltd, Trowbridge, Wilts, UK

Matador is an imprint of Troubador Publishing Ltd

This book is dedicated to my family
in recognition of their support over many years.

CONTENTS

FOREWORD

When in the autumn of 2003, and after the prompting of others, I decided to write my memoirs, I had no idea where the venture would take me; it was very much a journey into the unknown. I could not envisage necessarily how I would tackle it or how it would turn out. The exercise has been a bit like giving birth: a difficult and uncomfortable process at times, but with a highly satisfactory outcome.

And the outcome is a tale covering the 70 years of my life – both professional and domestic, private and public. The book uncovers many events and occasions, some of which came easily to mind, others buried more deeply in my memory bank.

I have to stress, straightaway, that this is not a definitive account of the Tullett businesses — in their various forms; neither is it an academic analysis of the money markets. It's how I see both and, in putting together this account, I have aimed for the greatest possible accuracy and trust that the combined force of my memory, other contributions and modern research techniques, have provided that. I apologise for any errors or omissions along the way. Bolted on to this narrative are my views, opinions and attitudes on a variety of subjects, for which I make no apologies!

Much has changed in the money markets during my 50 years there and I hope that, calling on all this experience, I have captured at least a flavour of life in the dealing rooms and the boardrooms. Perhaps to my surprise, I have enjoyed this process of revelation and hope that my energy and enthusiasm for so many things comes across on the page and offers an interesting read.

Finally, I should like to thank all those who made this book possible — those who contributed to the content, helped shape my approach, offered constructive suggestions, assisted with the editing and otherwise aided with its assembly. I'd like to make special mention of my family as well as, in no particular order: David Riley, Peter Doney, Alan Styant, David Clark, Michael Beales, Richard Magee, Terry Smeeton, Les and Jill Brock, David Lowe and Norman Hayden.

I make special mention above of those without whose contribution this book would not have been possible. However, as a final thought, I should like to thank all my friends and colleagues whose company and sociability I have had the good fortune to share down the years.

Derek Tullett
Keston
April 2007

I
THE DAY

The bedroom alarm clock burst into life, pulling me, as usual, from a pretty deep sleep. It was 5.50am, the usual time for me to wake up. Nothing about that surprised me. It seemed a normal enough start to a normal enough day — the like of which I had known for some forty-odd years. Each working day — and I'd never missed one through illness — had begun this way, offering that momentary pause for reflection before all hell let loose and beginning of the almighty struggle to get ready, followed by the dash to the station and the chance to join the other City souls in the headlong rush to be at my desk by 7.30am. Welcome to my world of work!

But as I cleared my eyes, and with it my head, I remembered suddenly that this was no normal day: no normal day by any stretch of the imagination. As I got up and took in the beautifully dawning spring day, with its unbelievably blue sky and surprisingly strong sunshine, I could only feel a huge sense of pride about what was ahead of me.

It was May 5, 1997 and I was off to Buckingham Palace to receive my CBE from Prince Charles. I certainly hadn't been able to take it in when I opened the letter some six months before, and I could scarcely do so now. From this moment I was seized by a vast sense of unreality that was to stay with me for much of the rest of the day. Indeed, all the experience and confidence that comes with an international business career could not have prepared me for this day, or these feelings. For once, I was nervous. Nervous that everything would pass off OK on one of the biggest occasions of my life, on one of the biggest stages imaginable.

A million or more thoughts queued up in my mind to await some form of processing. There was no time for that yet. Instead, I put my thoughts on hold and gave in to the practical needs of the moment. The four of us, my wife Anita and my two youngest sons, Jonathan and Kevin, had to be washed, breakfasted and kitted out within a couple of hours ready for Brian, my driver, to collect us and take us to the Palace.

Suddenly, the whole house was up, alive and full of activity and the usual scrum got under way, with bedrooms, bathrooms and the kitchen echoing to the sounds of people in a hurry. At one point, as I wrestled with my morning suit, I could hear Anita trying to reason with the boys, who were protesting: "But, where's my cufflinks and why do we have to wear this?" Most mornings were fraught enough, but this was in a league of its own. Jonathan kept up the pressure by announcing: "My hat's too big!" To which Anita, looking calm, composed and lovely in her apricot-coloured three-piece, responded: "Well, you only have to carry it." This he later did, until he didn't and decided to pose for the Palace photographers looking like a junior Eric Morecambe.

However, we made it out the other side of the most frantic session of getting ready you could imagine. Then, right on cue, Brian turned up with the office Jaguar and there we were — all scrubbed up, in our finest and, just as importantly, on time. So far, so good

Off we went from our home in Keston, Kent and it was a case of next stop Buck House, some 20 or so miles away. The

Big Day was under way. In the car, Anita began recounting the adventures she had had in finding a suitable outfit and for several miles thereafter there was much excited talk about what lay ahead. As the chatter filled the air and the car swept into suburban south London, my mood somehow changed: I drifted into thought and became altogether more contemplative. Here were streets that had been so familiar to me since early childhood. And, as I took this in, I began tapping into those thoughts that had craved my attention an hour or two earlier. It was as if the journey into town was to become an allegory of my life's journey so far.

Apart from the occasional nod in the direction of the cheery hubbub in the car, my gaze and thoughts were directed firmly out of the window — a window on my past. We moved through outer Croydon where I was brought up and on to Dulwich, where I was born. As we did so, the tree-laden streets blocked out the morning sun and brought an artificial darkness, which triggered sombre thoughts on my part.

So many memories came flooding back. Here I was on my way with my family to the crowning moment, in public terms at least, of a life that had brought commercial success, status and influence. And yet those early south London days could never have remotely suggested such a prospect. Little could I have imagined then that I would have come this far. The south London of the war years was uncertain and threatening — long on deprivation and short on optimism: days that were dominated by limited diets and dodging the ever-present danger from German air raids.

As we passed the tollgate near Dulwich College, I recalled the day that war broke out. I was five and living in Shirley near Croydon. But that fateful Sunday in early September 1939 my mother and I decided we would cycle over to Dulwich to see my grandmother. As we reached the tollgate, near the end of our journey, the air raid siren went off, a false alarm as it turned out. But the wailing that ripped through the air instilled fear into all of us for the first time on that warm, late summer lunchtime. It was a sound that would haunt Britons for the next six years.

I'd had a happy time before the war, but everybody's lives changed at that moment —11am on September 3, 1939. The hostilities and the broken families brought about by it totally dominated things. Normality was suspended for the duration. By now I was at Monks Orchard School in Shirley and the daily routine featured taking a case containing two biscuits and a bar of chocolate to aid survival in the shelters during an air raid. We got used to the raids in our area. Smashed windows were an almost daily occurrence as we dived for cover in the shelter built into the school. But one raid stood out vividly. That day the school got caught up in a Luftwaffe attack on a local industrial target called Muirheads, a plant where communications equipment was made. During the raid, the school playground was riddled with machinegun fire and pupils and teachers flung themselves to the ground in the chaos as the German fighters swooped low to strafe all they could see. How nobody was killed will remain a mystery forever. It was as amazing as it was frightening.

These were desperately worrying times. For a start, my father was abroad in the forces and, in common with all households throughout the country, we feared for his life. But after the attack on the playground my mother switched her concern to me and pleaded with me to leave London. I wasn't keen to be an evacuee but agreed to give it a go. In fact, I tried it for three weeks, hated it and was soon back with my mother happy to take my chance at school or in the Anderson shelter in our garden.

In those grim days you could not tell what the next day might bring, let alone contemplate the future. Growing up, having a career, getting married and starting a family seemed like the stuff of fiction, if not complete fantasy. Such ideas seemed faintly ridiculous when surviving each day was your sole concern. These were dark thoughts about what had been dark times ...

As I drifted back to the present and became more conscious of the journey, I'd hardly noticed our progress from the greenery of Dulwich into the familiar landmarks of central London. With the switch from the cool shade of the suburbs into the sunlit streets of the centre of town my mood lifted visibly as I contemplated happier days. The transformation represented the triumph of hope and ambition over adversity and despair. The uncertainties of wartime south London were now replaced by the post-war promise of the City. This was where I would make my fortune, bringing with it wealth, status and influence.

That I had followed a career in the City was possibly a surprise, if I thought about it. I had gone on to make my mark by building a company, which bore my name, and had turned it into the second biggest money broking house in the world. And that had led to this day of days. "For services to the financial markets ..." the CBE citation read. I kept turning the phrase over and over in my mind. "For services to the financial markets ..." How remote that would have seemed 58 years earlier to the boy whose only hankering had been to play sport and, possibly, design things. Well, there you go!

So, success in the City did surprise me. However, and this may sound arrogant, the fact that I had made such a success of something, did not. For I have always had a very determined streak in my character and I am sure I would have made the most of whatever path I had followed by working very hard at it.

By now, the car was bathed in sunshine as we approached Buckingham Palace and there was no chance of rain on my parade. After parking in the Mall, we left Brian with the car and took the short walk to the Palace. Passing through the gates at dead on 10am, I was fully back into the reality of the moment. And what a reality it was. Like a lot of people, I had seen pictures of the inside of Buckingham Palace on television or in newspapers or magazines. But few ever see the full splendour of its interior and get to meet a member of the Royal Family to boot.

It was thrilling for me, and equally so for Anita. Indeed, the excitement began for us both six months earlier when an unusual letter arrived at Keston while I was away on business in New York. As usual, Anita collected the post that day — but noticed that this particular letter stood out. Even with all the important mail that arrives for a businessman, it's not every day you get a letter from 10 Downing Street.

Anita didn't know what to make of it, so put it aside to await my return. On opening the letter, and for once in my life, I found myself speechless. I read it again, before calling to Anita: "Look at this!" Anita read it and discovered that I had been nominated for a CBE in the New Year's Honours. She flung her arms round me and said: "That's wonderful!" And, in a fit of masterly understatement, all I could think to say was: "I suppose it is."

Just two things were now required of us: a swift response and, if I accepted (as if there were any doubts!) the award had to be kept secret until it was formally announced in the list on January 1, 1997. As someone who does not show his emotions easily, keeping quiet has never been a problem. So, staying silent about the CBE didn't prove difficult. Anita and I wondered, instead, who had nominated me. We went through a list of suspects, but to this day we still don't know — although we have an inkling.

With purdah over, and with it our short spell of enforced silence, we threw a small dinner party for friends on New Year's

Eve and at midnight Anita brought in champagne and a marvellous cake inscribed: "Congratulations on your CBE!" It was our way of telling the world. And, of course, once the Honours List was published, the trickle of information was followed by a deluge of congratulatory letters. It was all rather humbling really.

Anita, the boys and I were now inside the Palace and the sheer grandeur of it all was somewhat overwhelming — yet we managed to retain an air of calm and the sense of occasion was not lost on any of us. Soon after entering the building, I was ushered to one side and Anita and the boys were directed to the magnificent main Ballroom where the families would watch the whole ceremony. Each recipient is allowed a maximum of three guests, so with around 130 award winners that day, there must have been audience of around 400.

With an orchestra playing softly in the background to provide a relaxed atmosphere, the Palace was a sight to behold. The stairways and hallways leading to the main rooms were decorated in white and gold with huge portraits lining each side. The Ballroom itself, the largest room in the palace, was a mixture of red, gold and white décor and boasted spectacular chandeliers along with a red carpet and red and gold chairs. This was one of 20 investitures hosted each year by the Palace, which sees 2,000 recipients filing through the building.

Ahead of me was a potentially long and nervous wait in the Picture Gallery. Celebrities and the not-so-well-known all rubbed shoulders as we were given a full briefing: where to stand, how to bow, retreat and where to go afterwards. Every question and request is catered for with officials pointing you in the right direction. It's brilliantly stage managed by military men bringing a military precision to the proceedings. Nothing's left to chance at Buckingham Palace on days like this and it's designed to calm the nerves.

We were addressed by Lieutenant Colonel Malcolm Ross, the Controller of the Lord Chamberlain's Office, who told us what we were required to do. At the same time we were urged to mix the business with pleasure. Just relax, he urged us, and you will enjoy and remember the day.

Armed with this nugget of information, we were then segregated and, at 11am on the dot, Prince Charles and a party, consisting of the Yeomen of the Guard in their splendid Tudor uniforms and two Ghurkha officers, entered the room and the ceremony proper began. The OBEs would go first, followed by MBEs with CBEs rounding off the show. So, I settled in my seat for the long wait and, looking around, noticed one or two familiar faces: the actor Michael York, athlete Jonathan Edwards and racing driver Damon Hill, were just some amid the throng.

But soon I was rescued from my nervous wait. It was my surname, of all things, which plucked me from what might have been an over-long ordeal. "Tu" — as in Tullett — was sitting next to "Va" — as in Vaughan and as in Frankie Vaughan the singer. What delightful company he turned out to be. We didn't know each other to begin with, but soon did. Like most other people at that time, I knew of his singing career on stage, screen and TV with a string of hit records in the 1950s, 60s and 70s, which brought him an adoring public and made him a household name.

But fame hid another side to Frankie Vaughan. Few knew of his devoted work for boys' clubs. I discovered that, totally belying his smooth showbusiness image, this lad from the backstreets of Liverpool had never forgotten his roots and made it his life's work to help youngsters from deprived backgrounds. He told me that when his Russian-Jewish family came to Britain he thought of becoming a boxer and later took up the sport at the Lancaster Boys' Club — so beginning a life-long connection with the boys' clubs movement. The many hours he put in supporting boys' clubs as a means of giving young men from poor areas a focus in life, had earned him an OBE in 1965 followed by the CBE for the same reason. A far cry from Hollywood and the West End — which is what I found fascinating about him, I think.

At long last the wait in the side room was over and suddenly the CBEs were on the move. I joined the queue of recipients, which snaked its way towards the main ballroom where Anita, Jonathan and Kevin were waiting with growing excitement for my moment. At least they had been able to watch the whole ceremony — from which I had been cut off.

We moved forward in groups of about 12 making our way to the Ballroom via a series of small galleries. Ahead in the Ballroom there was a dais to the left with the guests seated to the right. As we reached the door the Lord Chamberlain read out our name and award — at which point, of course, each recipient's family sat up to attention. Now, it was my turn. Although I like to think of myself as thoroughly modern in my approach to most things, I have to admit that British traditions – like the honours system – have their place. I considered it a great privilege to be chosen for a CBE and I was very proud to receive it.

As instructed, I walked forward to the dais where Prince Charles awaited and, my having bowed, he placed the insignia over my head and began talking to me. Having never met Frankie Vaughan before, it was ironic that I had actually been introduced to Prince Charles just a few months earlier. All this came about when I accepted an invitation from Lieutenant Colonel Sir Michael Gray to join other City financiers who were involved with the Airborne Charities, which looked after injured troops and their dependants. Then at a later function in Aldershot in connection with the charity, I met the prince in his capacity as colonel–in-chief of the Parachute Regiment.

Prince Charles recalled that meeting as we spoke. Certainly, it was a moment I will never forget as the prince, in a thoroughly professional way, created a marvellous air of informality in a highly-formal setting. He's only got a few seconds to talk to you, but goes out of his way to put you at ease. Then, following a handshake, I withdrew from the room as instructed and the CBE was taken from me and placed in a box.

I discovered later that as each person went up to Prince Charles, Anita and the boys craned their necks to see whether I was next. They were suitably impressed that my few words with the prince lasted longer than most of the other recipients. They also said they could sense my pride and humility from where they sat.

Within no time at all, the ceremony was over and I was able to rejoin Anita and the boys and emerged into the sunlight of the Buckingham Palace courtyard. After the pomp and dignity of the awards there followed what can only be described as an unseemly scrum as teams of photographers scrambled to get pictures of the award winners and their families, posing under green-and-white garden umbrellas in the great heat of that May day.

The photographs were to be treasured along with the video, I guess. But it all came at a price! Well, that's business for you.

Walking back through the gates towards the Mall and Brian, who was waiting with our car, I couldn't help but think that the crowds that gather outside for such occasions have a twin effect. On the one hand, they make you feel important. Yet, on the other hand, they help dispel the unreality of it all and bring you back down to earth.

It was time to move on and Brian whisked us around the corner from the Palace to lunch in one of my favourite haunts — the restaurant in the Lanesborough Hotel, on the site of the old St George's Hospital, Hyde Park Corner. The Lanesborough is a stylish hotel full of 19th century elegance with its dining room in the form of a conservatory — all delicate furniture and potted palms. Just right for the day.

Over lunch, I surprised Anita by giving her a special hand-made brooch, bearing a copy of the CBE insignia, which can only be presented to the spouse of a recipient. We were a very proud and happy family and I will always remember that Lanesborough lunch for that special sense of togetherness we enjoyed.

But our day was far from over. A fine meal and much champagne later, we headed home for an evening celebration with family and friends. On the way I tried to take in the day so far. For sheer exhilaration only two occasions previously could possibly have rivalled it. The first was returning from National Service in the Far East and seeing my parents and London again after such a long time away. The second, and entirely differently, was seeing Rudolf Nuryev and Margot Fontaine perform Swan Lake at Covent Garden on the opening night. Thrilling occasions all, but Buckingham Palace was clearly the tops.

Once home at Keston we unwound for the first time that day. We rounded off a superb, though hectic, few hours with a big thank-you to those people who had made my award possible – the business associates who had helped my career and the family and friends who had supported me in my endeavours. Ultimately, then, we had the pleasure of celebrating with those closest to me.

So, that May day turned out to be an enormous milestone in my life. A kaleidoscopic day of untold feelings and sensations that saw life images race through my head and brought with it an odd mixture of dark and light and pleasure and pain. But, most of all, it was a day for recalling what I had achieved — unimaginable in a childhood of rationing, air raids and hanging on for dear life — and to draw breath and, even in my sixties, to look forward to the challenges that undoubtedly lay ahead for me.

2

THE BEGINNING

Friern Road, Dulwich was full of worthy, but rather nondescript, terraced houses much loved by aspirational middle-class families in the 1930s. And my family was no different. My parents, Percy and Vera Tullett (my mother's family name was Flatman), were Londoners and, indeed, both sets of grandparents lived nearby in Herne Hill and South Norwood in South London.

My father's principal work was as a wholesale importer/exporter of vegetables and fruit. He started off in partnership with John Luttmer, a well-known company, and they imported around 60% of the onions that came into the UK, mostly from Holland. They had a business near The Monument, alongside London Bridge, which served the Covent Garden, Spitalfields and Borough markets. Many years later my father joined a company in Covent Garden whose premises is now a unisex hairdressers (I think my father would turn in his grave if he knew that!).

Working in the markets was a very demanding job with long hours. My father had to get up incredibly early six mornings a week to go to the market and, some years later, I got a taste of this by going to work with him on the occasional Saturday.

The first major event of my childhood that I recall was moving in 1937 from Dulwich to 53, Ash Tree Way, Shirley near Croydon. The next two years proved to be a relatively tranquil time at home with my parents before the fury of war hit my young life with a vengeance.

We lived in a good three-bedroom house in a private area near The Glades in Shirley. It was the type of house you would expect in an area full of young, middle-class couples just starting families. My father, being a talented artist, decorated my bedroom with drawings and paintings of Walt Disney's characters Mickey Mouse and Pluto. He also put these talents to good use when he was away at war by sending home letters beautifully illustrated with scenes from where he was based. It helped lighten the many dark days of the war.

Shirley was a pleasant area with decent neighbours, who were to really show their mettle during the blitz. At home, we had a reasonable-sized garden and you could certainly get a cricket pitch in it and where we also used to play football. As we lived fairly near a recently-closed golf course at Addiscombe we played there, too. So, we had plenty of spaces to play in.

These were happy days and, despite being an only child, I didn't want for company and had lots of friends to play with. I was close to both my parents, but displayed an early independence and tried to make decisions for myself. And as a fully-paid-up member of the awkward squad, I was to show time and again that I'd sooner make the wrong decision myself than have somebody else make the right decision for me.

Even at a very early age, too, I was never a romantic, always a realist — which, perhaps, offers a clue to my personality. In fact, I was one of those annoying children that always questioned things. "Why are you saying that?" "Where do you get those facts from?" In my grammar school days I was to become a staunch supporter of the Labour Party, while my parents were to the right of Genghis Khan! This was as contrary as it gets and led to many lively mealtimes!

Life, then, jogged along and up to the summer 1939 all seemed well in the Tullett cosmos. However, September 3 was to bring a huge double change to my life. Soon after that fateful date my father joined the forces and went off to war and, so, disappeared from the lives of my mother and myself for the next six years. This was a massive wrench and caused a severe hiatus in our family relationships — as we were to discover when my father returned in 1945. Neither my mother nor myself could say we really knew him and, clearly, a lot of catching up would be needed.

For now, my mother had to dig deep and learn how to cope without him. Before they married she had worked as a secretary at the Army & Navy Stores in Victoria, but left work when she was pregnant with me and had settled into the comfortable life of a housewife. But the war brought a new landscape and, shorn of my father's peacetime income, life was difficult. She couldn't live on a soldier's allowance and to make ends meet, my mother took a job with an insurance company in central London. With my father away, I inevitably spent a lot of time with my mother and it made us close, but not overly so.

Coinciding with my father's departure there was another huge transformation in my life. Being five years old, I had reached the traditional childhood landmark of going to school for the first time. In my case, it was Monks Orchard School. But before I could really get to grips with this new environment, I had an even more difficult situation to deal with — evacuation to the countryside.

It was my mother's decision that I should be evacuated, though it would prove to be a very short spell apart from her. She thought it was in my best interests to be safely away from the London area. But after just a few weeks I was to return when my mother's loneliness and vulnerability — with my father abroad — proved too much for both of us. But such an unlikely outcome was far from my thoughts as I turned up at Waterloo Station with other local Croydon children bound for Wiltshire. While nervous and upset at the thought of being parted from my mother, I remember thinking how well organised the whole thing was. The steam train journey down to Wiltshire was pretty uneventful, except that I marvelled at how green everything was and that I had never been so far into the countryside.

I was met at my destination by a rather pleasant family who worked a smallholding. I cannot recall their names or what town or village I was in, but I do know that I settled in pretty well and soon began to relish the fresh air and being in the country. I also became good friends with the couple's son and I enjoyed the school I was attending.

During my five weeks there my mother visited me twice and, although she was reluctant to say so, it soon became obvious that we missed each other a lot. I had this overwhelming feeling that my place was with her and that I should return home to Croydon where I could also be re-united with my friends. Taking a five-year-old away from its mother for the first time is always a traumatic experience. For me, it was the latest in a terrifying set of circumstances for a youngster: the physical threat of war, seeing my father disappear into the forces and then being torn from my mother, my home, my friends and my school and transplanted many miles away.

It's clear that evacuation did suit some people — particularly as the bombing of Britain's major cities continued for most of the war. Many evacuees liked it enough that, when the war ended, they chose to stay in their new environment, rather than return to their homes. But this world was not for me and after I told my mother of my decision, she contacted the authorities and the next thing I knew I was on a train back to London where I resumed my schooling at Monks Orchard.

Obviously, these were no ordinary school days with air raids dominating our lives. Each day as you arrived at school you wondered what danger you would face and worrying whether your house would be there when you got home. And as I've recalled earlier the most terrifying and never-to-be-forgotten moment of the lot, of course, was the Luftwaffe machine-gunning of the playground.

But even on ordinary days, the biggest single decision we had to make was simply what to do when the dreaded air raid siren sounded. Should we run to the shelter or dive for cover wherever we could?

Even if you were at home, the dilemma was the same: should you go down into the shelter or seek refuge under the special reinforced metal table, designed to take the weight of the debris, which the authorities had provided? Opinion, even within families, could be split on this. We lived in a small terrace of houses and, at one stage, all the mothers decided to pool their skills and build an Anderson shelter across the front gardens. They felt it was safer for children than being under the metal table — known as the Morrison shelter — in each house. I remember disagreeing, believing that if anything fell on that table it wouldn't be destroyed and you'd have air to breathe.

At other times we braved the raids outside. Late in the war, I recall standing quite casually in our back garden and watching the totally-deadly V1 bombs heading for their targets in London and surrounding areas like Croydon. Then there were the frightening V2s, which used to fly over and, when the engine cut out, drop without any noise. Even if they stopped in flight a couple of miles away, you felt you had to rush inside and get under the table, just in case. Incendiary bombs were also a big problem for us in the early part of the war and some houses in our small road were destroyed by them in the fire storm they created.

Sometimes a raid caught you when you were away from the safety of the shelters or a building. If the siren sounded while we were playing in the fields, we often stayed put — believing that the woods were as safe as anywhere at those moments.

Air raids apart, life still managed to throw up some happy moments. Yes, times were tough, but they were friendly, too. I loved sport and my friends and I were always to be found on our playing fields — now a council estate— making our own fun, our own sport. We played cricket and football and ran races, much like youngsters do. And, as all small children would expect, even in wartime, life had its treats. Endless summer hours were spent in the local park and, from time to time, my mother and I managed a break from London. We took the train down to the coast and to Worthing and Broadstairs — but a favourite destination of mine, was Hastings. Perhaps it was because friends of ours used to have a caravan there and we often stayed in it for a week or so. I remember going to the Isle of Wight at some stage as well.

Hobbies also managed to flourish in wartime. Influenced, perhaps, by my father, I was proving to be something of an artist — a talent that school certainly helped me develop. I mainly did still-life watercolours because oils just weren't available given the wartime shortages. And each month, stumbling through London's bomb craters and rubble, my mother used to take me to the art galleries and to a theatre in the West End. She saw these trips as part of my upbringing and my love of the stage began then and has remained with me ever since.

By and large, we had a fairly healthy life — made the more so, in my opinion, by the fact that food was rationed and you had to eat carefully. We tried to help both ourselves and the community at large by doing our bit — for example, my mother grew lettuce and our nextdoor neighbours kept chickens, which we shared. Things like that created social cohesion and a togetherness among people that was unique to that time.

Overall, I think the war years gave me a number of things. On the surface it saw the development of what has become a lifelong interest in sport and a childhood fascination with the idea of design. But deeper down, and more fundamentally, those years created in me — and many other youngsters at the time — a toughness and resilience that was to be central to my character and which I was to put to good use in my business career.

The wartime experience taught you to look after yourself: this gave you a discipline and a lot of self-confidence. Emerging from the war as a young child you felt that if you could survive that you could survive anything. Certainly a lot of my friends from those days later emerged with a robust spirit and, like me, started businesses and made fair successes of them. All things considered, it was a childhood that you would not have necessarily chosen; it was a childhood that the war chose for you.

As peace returned in 1945, I experienced double excitement. Firstly, I saw my soldier-father again. He had been away for practically the whole of the war with the Queen's Royal Regiment in Egypt and later in Italy and in France just after D Day. Then during my final days in the summer term at Monk's Orchard, he strode into the school hall and, rather poignantly, I didn't recognise him. The headmistress said: "Would Derek Tullett please stand up." And my father said: "I can't believe that you are up to here, the last time I saw you, you were up to here". It was a very emotional moment for us both. Having been close to him until I was five, my father had become, inevitably, a rather distant figure. Being brought up by my mother on her own had felt normal enough — simply because all my friends, with their fathers away, too, had experienced this. Every child was the same: we'd been through the same things and had the same problems. This gave us a great sense of togetherness.

Even with a war on, education had not stood still and soon it was time to leave Monks Orchard. By some divine intervention, I had won a scholarship to Whitgift School, Croydon, which came as a big surprise and a great thrill. I was one of two boys who transferred there from Monk's Orchard: the other was Arthur Bateman, a much brighter pupil than me, who later made his fortune in advertising and last heard of in Australia.

Not surprisingly, the close friendships made at Monks Orchard didn't really survive the switch to Whitgift at the age of 11 and I never really had contact with them again. The exception is John Surtees who was to ride to fame as a motorcyclist and racing driver in the 1960s and 70s. He later became a successful businessman and, having been in touch with him in the early part of this year, understand he is becoming involved in motor sport administration. In contrast to the Monks Orchard experience, I am still close to boys from Whitgift days — easily understandable, I suppose. After all, you spend more years with your school friends at that stage and when you leave you are all emerging into the outside world verging on adulthood.

I can clearly remember my first day at Whitgift. My mother took me to school but I wouldn't let her go with me up the drive to the building. I walked the last bit by myself dressed in the full school uniform of short trousers, cap and tie. The building looked much as it does today and, to a young impressionable boy, it seemed physically intimidating — possessing a grand edifice that housed, I was to discover, years of scholarship and tradition. There were four forms in the first year and there were around 30 boys in my class. Ahead of me were the seconds, thirds, fourths, removed fifths and sixth.

So began a near life-long affection for a school with which I am still closely involved today. I guess the thing that proved important to me at Whitgift was the fact that I was a rather prolific sportsman — good at athletics, rugby, boxing, hockey and squash and not a bad cricketer, either. Rugby was a strange one for me because I'd never played the game until I got to Whitgift. But I had a natural eye for ball games, so I soon learned the game and how to play it. I suppose you could say I was something of an all-round sportsman, which made me reasonably popular with the other boys.

Sportsmen had a great time at Whitgift. It was, very obviously, a very sporting school whose head at the time was the father of Robin Marler, who was to play cricket for Sussex and England and later became a well-known cricket writer. In those days we played against schools like Dulwich College, Judd's, Tonbridge, St John's, Leatherhead and King's College, Wimbledon. The one thing I was sorry to have missed out on was fencing, which, in my view, is one of the great sports.

Apart from sport, I excelled at mathematics, which has always come easy to me. Mathematics requires logical thinking and, along with my pronounced independence, led me to question everything and be inquisitive about everything — which must have been maddening for my teachers. I had an inherent talent for maths — my father was a good mathematician and had a great capacity for mental arithmetic. In turn, my sons have good mathematical brains which they have used in their various careers. A lot of people are employed in the money markets today because they have studied quantitative mathematics at university and think logically.

Oddly enough, it was my ability at maths, as well as a talent for art, that led me to ponder a career not in the money markets, but in design and technology. That sort of work and possibly advertising — very much in its infancy in Britain in those days — appealed to me then.

My passion for art, nurtured by my good-humoured art master Frank Potter, made me feel quite creative. And I began design drawing in charcoal — with other materials hard to come by — in a draughtsman-cum-Leonardo da Vinci sort of way.

For example, I would look at house plans and re-design them. As for making design a career when I left school, I guess the idea just faded away. But my love of painting has remained with me and I am a keen collector of art.

Elsewhere in the classroom, I was good at physics, but would say I was average at all other subjects. My form master in those days was a great character called Freddie Percy, a very famous Old Whitgiftian, who also taught me rugby. Freddie, who died recently in his nineties, has written books on Whitgift, as well as being the school's archivist for years. Indeed, he would trawl the Honours List for Old Whitgiftians whose names could be mentioned in the Whitgift magazine.

At the school with me was Raman Subba Row, who went on to play cricket for Surrey and became an England batsman and, later a Test selector. Also there was David Hancock, later knighted, who became permanent secretary to the Department of Education and Ian Beer, also knighted, who was the epitome of the perfect public school boy. Ian was regimental sergeant major in the cadet force, sang the lead in all the operas, played the lead in all the dramas and captained the school rugby team. He went up to Cambridge, captained them at rugby and then played for England. Ian was to have a distinguished career as a headmaster of three independent schools, including Lancing and Harrow, and was prominent in other areas of public life. Ian's a charming person and does a lot of work for charity. We played old boy rugby together for years and I remember how, in gathering old age, we used to arrive early to bandage ourselves up.

Life at Whitgift was enriched in a number of other ways. The school had a strong combined cadet force led, of course, by Ian Beer, and which I was keen to join. I recall some great times at camp and the experience formed a good base for my later National Service. In addition, Whitgift always had a huge range of extra-mural activities: we had a poetry society, debating society, chess club, drama group and orchestra. Boys were well catered for this way, so helping to civilise them and give them a hinterland of interests to be called on in later life.

What else do I recall of Whitgift in those bleak post-war days? In the first year I used to travel to school by bus but later took to cycling as there wasn't much traffic on the roads and the journey was only 30 minutes. I remember, too, that the school uniform was compulsory and that in summer we wore straw boaters. If I think about it, it must have been something of a financial burden for my parents to pay for all that clothing and the sports kit in particular.

Physically, the Whitgift of today has only really changed in terms of an extension to the main building. Just after the war there were about 850 boys there, now there are 1,100. Then it was a state grammar school; today it's totally independent. I got a scholarship then, today they have their own bursaries etc. Over the years I've been involved with the school in a variety of ways, which I will describe in a later chapter.

The next milestone for me at school was taking the leaving exams. It was 1951, I was 17, and we were just changing from matriculation to GCEs. I never ever thought of staying on. Very few people went to university, most people went into National Service. As I could see no end to National Service — which didn't finish until the late fifties, as it happens – and, as I didn't want to go to university, I decided to get my two years out of the way and get on with the rest of my life.

Two years later I left Whitgift bound for the Army via a short, but useful, detour. While National Service may have come as a shock to many young men of that era, I was quite prepared for it. After all, my father and uncle had been in the Army, as had both my grandfathers in the First World War, and I had been in the school Combined Cadet Force, so it didn't hold any terrors for me.

But, before I reported for duty, something happened which, looking back, proved to be a seminal moment. My mother, being an intensely practical person, suggested — nay, insisted — that I look beyond the forces and work for three months to get a feel for the world of commerce. My mother suggested I spend some time at the Australia & New Zealand Bank. She realised that if you did a short spell with the company beforehand you could come straight out of the Army back into a job. The senior figure there — in fact, its personnel director — was Bernard Searle, an Old Whitgiftian, who was always happy to recruit old boys. The school's old boys always helped each other out in such ways.

So, I went there with a Whitgift friend of mine and, true enough, when we finished our National Service we both went back. Despite my mother's best endeavours, I was to dislike both spells at the bank, but it was very useful in introducing me to the world of finance and confirming for me what I didn't want to do. It also proved an introduction to the dealing room, which I most definitely did want to do.

Digressing, I would say that although my parents were closely involved in this move — one which proved important as it gave me an insight into the world of finance— it wasn't typical of their approach at the time. They were generally non-interventionist in my schooling or in decisions about possible careers. They were a somewhat "eccentric" couple who never really talked to me about such things: and they certainly didn't try to guide me. What is more, I think I have inherited this laid-back style: I've adopted the same approach with my four sons — who have grown up to be great boys. Over the years I've never tried to influence or encourage them to do anything one way or another.

Anyway, after three months at the bank I began my two years' National Service spending six weeks training at Stoughton Barracks in Guildford, after which I wasn't to see my parents again until I left the Army. The training was tough going, but necessary and excellent because it made you so fit at the end of it. Fortunately, I always approved of drill and when I later became a platoon commander I could see that if you shouted the order correctly the troops under you would react instantly and without question. That's actually what you need from an infantryman, in particular. In training I'd already started to formulate my ideas about leadership.

Next it was Germany for further training before being sent out to Malaya, via Aden and Singapore, and plunged into the teeth of the emergency there as a 19-year-old platoon commander in the Queen's Royal Regiment, which all male soldiers in my family have served in.

I had my first taste of jungle warfare, which our excellent training enabled us to deal with. Britain, after all, had had many years of practice in this type of guerilla war.

I think that what I liked most about those days was the tremendous fellowship. They were difficult times, but we had a lot of laughs and a few tears together. Thankfully, it wasn't all action and with sport being important in the Army, I boxed and played rugby for the regiment. However, some people got to the stage where they couldn't take it any more but were protected, which was correct.

They weren't sent away or anything like that; they were just given a role that took them away from the frontline and didn't involve them in the "nasties". My first real "nasty" came towards the end of my time in Malaya. I was commanding a small patrol near Tampin when I had my first experience of killing. We engaged a terrorist gang — killing two gang members and wounding another. I was commended for my part in the action but it was quite a sobering experience.

What I liked least about service life was the poor decisions taken about the leadership. If you were a public schoolboy you were an officer; that was a fact. But I felt that was wrong because, while I worked with three or four fantastic officers, far too many were too weak to hold such a position. They simply didn't have the capacity to do the job. Of course, a lot of men who could do the job never got the chance. And that's wrong, too.

There were parts I didn't like about my Army days and I became a bit disillusioned. So much so, that I wrote a letter to The Times saying what the hell were thousands of troops doing 7,000 miles from home chasing 500 communist terrorists, with the local Malayan people hating us. Of course, with hindsight, I can see that this is the plight of all occupying forces, before and since — and we were no different. Anyway, I showed the letter to my commander in chief, who, strangely enough, said that he agreed with me. But he could not allow me to have the letter published.

All things considered, I think the biggest thing I took from those two years was an early lesson in leadership and man management. There are two types of men in the Army: those who want to lead and those who want to be led. I wanted to lead, which the Army allowed me to do. And I found myself in charge of young men who, quite simply, didn't want to be there. The experience I gained in organisation and leadership formed the basis of my management style in later years.

One way or another, then, the Army proved to be an education and more useful to me than university might have been. On one level it had made me professionally ambitious — while abroad I had studied for an external degree through the London school of Economics. On another level, it gave me qualities that I was able to take forward into later life, not least the ability to be brave which jungle warfare certainly taught me.

There was a lot that happened in Malaya and later in Korea which, to this day, I'm not allowed to discuss. Sufficient to say, I finished up, officially, as a corporal. But, in practice, I was an acting lieutenant, which was slightly unusual. I did, on a couple of occasions, consider fleetingly whether to accept a commission and stay on in the regular Army, but I decided against it and so life as a civilian beckoned.

3

THE ARRIVAL

On returning to Britain, I took up the option of going back to the Australia and New Zealand Bank. The prospect didn't exactly set my pulse racing, but it was a job at least. It hadn't pressed any buttons for me in my first spell and nothing was to change this time around. Six months down the line I was to decide to leave because it clearly wasn't for me. My mother wasn't impressed with this and I remember her saying to me: "You know what you're giving up, don't you"? To which I replied: "No, what am I giving up? "A thousand pounds a year and a pension!" "OK mum, I'm quite happy to give that up. It doesn't matter, I'm off!"

Although bank life wasn't for me, this second spell at A&NZ did offer something different. I would discover three big compensations about being there. Firstly, the offices on the ground floor of a building in Cornhill in the City possessed a lovely banking hall — which was attractive to the eye and well worth a visit. Secondly, I made some good friends and contacts, particularly the bank's chief dealer, who was an Old Whitgiftian, with whom I was to stay in touch until his death. Thirdly, I was very lucky to have been put on to the trading floor, where I learned a lot that helped point me in the direction of money broking.

Up to that point money broking had been a closed book to me. I had no idea about its background and what it was. In fact, there has been money broking in Britain for at least 100 years, but the modern markets have only really taken shape since 1945 and, more particularly, since the 1970s. In fact, it was only in the 1950s that broking really got going again after the markets had closed during the war. Although modern broking is heavily defined by the technology that has put the world at the end of a phone or a computer, the job has not really changed in its essentials to those that greeted me in the mid-50s.

The money markets are made up of brokers and dealers. The dealers in the banks and other major financial houses are the actual buyers and sellers of currency in the market. It is the broker's job to collect and disseminate information, interpret it and then decide how, where and when to use it. This information creates a centralised price at which dealers at the client banks can transact business. In other words, a broker is a middle-man or facilitator: if he gets an offer, he puts it into the market and if he gets a bid he has a two-way market which he then spreads around the market. Brokers must not act as principals and deal on their own account.

A broker gets information from vendors, the media, government figures, official statements or, even, mere word of mouth. All day long new information is sought and translated into new prices. The money markets move at astonishing speed and it is vital that a broker possesses the skills of speed and accuracy to be able to keep up with the game. A young broker will rely heavily on his personality to gain business. I was to discover that as brokers mature, they gain greater technical knowledge which promotes better business.

Generally speaking, the quality of a broker's business will be based on the quality of service on offer in a series of markets. Ultimately, clients must be sure about what they are getting, to the point where the broker can assure them: "It's what it says on the tin". At the time I entered the industry, there were just 12 broking firms in London and they were restricted to just two markets — what is called "spot" and "forwards" in dollars against sterling and sterling against other currencies. The spot market is where currency is bought and sold for immediate delivery; whereas forwards deals — based on the relationship of interest rates — are where it is agreed to purchase or sell the underlying currency at a predetermined exchange rate — as a result of which a margin of risk exists until the date the forward matures.

Anyway, I managed to get into broking as part of a general introductory experience for new recruits at A&NZ and learned a lot from some very skilful traders. I worked first on the accountancy side in the back office and went from there into the dealing room proper. And I took to it straight away. My initial role was to "clear up" the day's deals. If, towards the end of the day, we had out-trades, it was my job to sort these out and tidy things up so that we didn't have currency deficits on the books.

I had, if you like, a general role without any specific responsibility, but it gave me a first taste of broking — which, as a young man in the grey days of post-war London, I saw as something rather exotic, something rather exciting. Not only did I enjoy the day-to-day work, but also I could foresee growth in the broking market that would follow the development of the banks and that the job would become "sexy" and richly rewarded.

It was also obvious to me that the regulation that stopped brokers dealing outside London would have to go, which would bring about other great opportunities. In fact, this limited market continued until 1966 when Harold Wilson's Labour government relaxed the rules and opened things up and the markets took a giant step forward and never looked back again.

A further bonus for me was the colourful world I stumbled

upon. There were real characters in the dealing room. One was Jimmy Warwick, an excellent trader: relaxed, analytical and popular in the market. Jimmy's leadership was crucial in the early days and his talents were universally recognised. Another key figure was Jack Liddel who was poached as Chief Dealer from William & Glyn's, something that was almost unheard of in the 1950s.

Another character was a very bright, but eccentric, dealer called Ken Wilkes who impressed me greatly. He had odd habits — one of which was his rather startling and impressive decision to do a German newspaper crossword in German! Ken was also a bit of a one-off where work was concerned. One day he arrived at the office brandishing a logo machine he had bought on behalf of the bank for £2,000, a lot of money then, which he believed would make our fortunes. It was a device for calculating currency changes, which I believe was a first.

"This is the way we are going to make money," he announced with delight. The machine was a big, round drum, which was operated, basically, like a giant slide rule. Little did we know that this rather primitive-looking contraption, which was quite complex in its way, would prove important for two reasons. It was the first advance on the then state-of-the-art technology of adding machines; but, more significantly, it was the first form of computer-driven thinking used in the markets. Certainly it was complex enough to baffle most of us and only Ken truly understood its workings, however hard he tried to explain it to his colleagues!

The theory was this: a lot of business was done in short-date Canadian/US dollar swaps which was done one-eighth either side of par — that is, trading one-eighth premium and one-eighth discount. Ken reckoned that with his machine he could work out currency movements days and months in advance, so potentially making a killing.

Launch day arrived and he roped me into the money machine's first outing. My job was to be his position keeper — which meant, I had to keep his position open using the money made available for placing that day, or vice versa. After about two hours I looked at the deals that I was putting through and approached Ken with a sense of trepidation. "Excuse me, sir," I said. "Go away," he snorted in a Dickensian manner. "I'm too busy, just get on with it. I'm going to put so many deals on. I'm making so much money." To which, I then implored: "No, please don't!" But, he ignored my pleadings and did more and more business.

A further hour on, I couldn't stand it any more and approached him again. "Mr Wilkes I have to speak to you." He relented. "Well what is it?" I then told him the bad news. "Every deal you've done this morning you've made a loss on." "No, I can't have done," he retorted. With a sense of disbelief, he put everything down and came over to check. "My God, I have!" he cried. In my role as calculator of the trades, it had become obvious that — when we converted back into US dollars — we were dealing on the wrong side of the market each time.

This device had proved very expensive. Ken had lost £10,000 that morning via a machine that he'd bought for £2,000. The dealing room had to pick up the £12,000 bill and as first-day disasters go, this was up there with the best of them. After such a debacle, there was, as you can imagine, a lack of confidence surrounding Ken's "money maker". But despite that inglorious start and the touch of ritual humiliation that it brought him, Ken Wilkes was convinced his principal was correct and that he had the right technology to go with it — it's just that he had got it the wrong way round! Quite simply, he had misused the slide rule. This led to the machine being mothballed. But when the slide rule problem was sorted out, the machine proved very effective and a great testimony to Ken Wilkes' ingenuity.

The Wilkes' episode certainly created a real stir. His machine had introduced possibilities for high-precision trading positions the like of which the markets had never seen. For example, the markets had real problems with the idea of trading in currencies one-eighth either side of par. Nobody was remotely sure what this really meant. It caused much debate, most memorably at one dinner in the City when one member, a bit the worse for wear, got up to respond to a question: "We must have una … unanim … unanimity!" he insisted, only to fall off his seat as he attempted to sit down!

Eventually, it was decided to re-write the terminology in the Bank of England's manual and from then on everybody wanting to trade in this way had to say: "I wish to buy Canadian dollars one-eighth in my favour." And it's no exaggeration to say that such a change in terminology proved to be one of the foundations of the modern market. The dealing room, inevitably, is a somewhat closed world with its own language, but it's vital to have clear terminology so that nobody is in any doubt about what you mean — this creates confidence, which is the bedrock of a sound market.

Ken Wilkes is, then, an important footnote in the history of the money markets. By the time he left A&NZ, technology had moved on and his machine sat on the side of the office resembling something of a museum piece. After I left, I kept in touch with the bank for several years and every time I went into the dealing room there was the Wilkes machine — without doubt, though, it was the forerunner of the more sophisticated technology to come.

My dealing room experience — and particularly the Wilkes episode — taught me two things: it showed me there was money to be made, but that I needed to go elsewhere to do it. I realised, quite simply, that my future did not lie with A&NZ. I detected in my short time there a distinct lack of opportunity. The bank management was in the form of a hierarchy: you couldn't skip a step in order to get on and each hurdle had to be negotiated laboriously — a bit like the old Civil Service where somebody had to move on, before you could. That wasn't for me. I guess my impatience was a sort of legacy from the leadership "kick" I experienced in my Army days. I didn't want to wait 20 years before becoming a bank manager: it wasn't on my agenda at all.

So, after five months, I decided to leave and began looking around for a better opportunity. A&NZ had a high profile in the market and, although I had no seniority there, I was able to meet and talk to brokers in the trading room and so was able to put my wares in the shop window. What is more, one company, Savage & Heath, put it to me that I was developing something of a reputation and that I should think of becoming a broker? "Well, why not?" I thought. I was quite happy to try. I didn't expect a contract, but was keen to know what I'd be paid, not that it would have made any difference. To my great delight, it turned out to be twice what I was earning at the bank!

I left A&NZ very amicably, however. They gave me a terrific leaving present, in the form of a silver cutlery service, and the friendships made — such as the colleagues who, along with me, formed a jazz band to play at evening and weekend functions — lasted way beyond my time there.

In 1955, therefore, just short of my 21st birthday and armed with Part 1 of the banking exams, (I knew I didn't need Part 2 where I was going), I headed for Savage & Heath determined to make a success of money broking.

What awaited me there? S&H came about as a result of one of the many mergers in the post-war money markets, which saw the number of broking houses reduced considerably from the 32 that existed in the 1930s. And I certainly wasn't put off by the remarks of a friend who took me aside at my 21st birthday party. "That's a difficult company you're joining!" he confided. I suppose he meant that it was rather small and something of a niche operation — which, actually, suited me. Whereas A&NZ had been too big for me, the "smallness" of Savage & Heath rather appealed.

As I say, I believed broking would grow and small firms would grow within it. But I could see this could be difficult for firms like S&H. After all, such growth might require a period during which all the profits might need to be ploughed back into the company to take it forward. And with brokers working on fixed commissions —to remain the case for another 30 years — this was tricky and expensive for small firms, which had to employ enough staff to be able to offer a proper service to customers, while remaining competitive and at the forefront of the market.

These were problematic, yet challenging, thoughts — but they were for the future and certainly not uppermost in my mind as I arrived for my new job. Our offices were above the Jamaica Inn just off Cornhill and, of course, the Jamaica became our second home and where much of the client entertaining went on. In those days, client entertainment was essential and took up a fair bit of the company's revenues, even though it was on a far smaller scale than before the war when there were some excesses.

The money market I had joined was basically made up of the brokers who had operated since before the war in the shadow of the Royal Exchange. During the 1950s, the Bank of England invited some of the old brokers to return and to set up a broking system based on the Bank's foreign exchange controls.

Each of the market's 12 broking companies had their own geographical "territory" and the area near Cornhill was S&H's patch. Our premises in Throgmorton Avenue looked a bit jaded and badly in need of a makeover. In addition, we only had 10 dealer boards — compared with today, when in some broking rooms, 1,000 boards are common along with all the technology you could possibly want.

As it happens, both the firm's founders — Peter Savage and Bill Heath — were still there when I joined. They were very much the old-style, larger-than-life "personality" brokers who got business through social, often old school, contacts. The partners were good at what they did and what they did was based on what they knew. As personality brokers, typical of pre-war broking in London, they gained all business by lavishly entertaining old friends. They never went out to secure accounts — this approach became the province of newcomers like myself, who were the first wave of a more meritocratic intake that was in full flood by the late 70s and early 80s.

Peter Savage was a tiny, round man and horse racing was his big thing. Each afternoon, there was a lot of contact with the bookmakers and, if things were especially quiet, he'd slip away to a race meeting close to London. He used to say to Mrs Bailey, who did all the accounts: "Is there any money in petty cash? I think I might go down to Kempton Park." And off he'd go.

I'd only been there about six weeks when Peter died. Quite naturally, his death caused a real hiatus in a company with only six staff. When it came to sorting out the partnership there was a disagreement with Peter's wife about how much it was all worth. Of course, Peter's death also offered a unique and early opportunity for me to progress, as Peter's accounts — or lines of business, as they are known — came up for grabs.

For his part, Bill Heath was a public schoolboy, a good broker and a real nice guy. He was a fine rugby player — No 8 for Richmond in his day — and a great raconteur and stories about him abound. One day he apparently arrived at the office dressed in his morning suit with his trousers badly torn and covered in mud. "Are you all right Mr Heath?" concerned colleagues enquired, to which Bill replied a little uncertainly:

"Had a few to drink last night. Got down to the house, walked down the driveway to the house and realised it was the wrong house. So, I turned and thought I won't go further. I walked through all the gardens as I couldn't be bothered to go back out. I got up this morning and had a headache. I just put the clothes on that I had taken off last night. I'm a bit of a mess aren't I?"

The third S&H partner was Ginger Weedon, another great character and the subject of many stories also. One concerned his next-door neighbour, a well-known financial journalist of the time. One day they were travelling home together when they got talking about gardening. The neighbour asked Ginger: "How do you grow such good tomatoes?" Ginger replied: "Actually, there's a secret to it — you just apply some urine to them."

So, the journalist went straight home and peed over his tomatoes, but by the next morning they were stone dead. When he next saw Ginger, he confronted him, saying: "That wasn't good advice" "What did you do?" enquired Ginger. "I peed all over them," said the journalist. "Ah well, sorry old chap, I forgot to tell you it's actually a tablespoon of the stuff to two gallons of water!"

The fourth partner was Val Edwards, whose two sons Michael and Brian were later to join the business. When I joined S&H I was living in Kenley near Purley and travelled to town each day with Val, who lived in Caterham. Val would wear his curly bowler and his black suit, and carry an umbrella and a copy of The Times. I resisted this uniform and simply wore a dark suit.

However, the one thing Val insisted upon was that I travelled first class on the train with him. He used to say: "When the inspector comes round I'll pay him". In those days first class rail travellers had their own seats and nobody would dare sit in yours. One morning, though, Val's image took a bit of knock when, after his usual "Morning gentleman" as he entered the compartment, he put his hat and umbrella on the luggage rack and opened his Times only to discover that his children had been tampering with it. Out fell copies of The Beano and The Dandy. "OK Val? What are you reading today?" the rest of the compartment chorused in delight.

Understandably, as a small company, S&H kept a close eye on its spending — but mainly in the wrong areas! Penny pinching was at its worst in our surroundings. We had modest looking, but reasonably-sized, premises and the problem was the partners never saw fit to improve them. This created a poor impression for clients who came in, looked around and concluded the place was a bit shabby — which must have influenced their opinion of our capabilities, too.

One weekend I decided I could not stand it any longer. With the help of two colleagues, I painted the place. During our work we came across all sorts of odd things. For a start, Bill Heath had a massive old mahogany stand in the hall with a mirror in the middle — something that probably didn't fit into his house. To achieve some of our makeover we had to cut off the top piece. When Bill came in on the Monday and saw what had happened, he exclaimed: "It's worth a lot of money!" "Yes it was, but it's not now," was all I could think to say.

Another example of cost-cutting came at Christmas when the firm steadfastly refused to foot the bill for the brokers to take their clients out for a meal. So, we entertained them at Throgmorton Avenue and had a sort of cover made for the dealer boards — used in conjunction with telephones to conduct our business each day — so that we could serve drinks to our guests.

But business was good and we soon started to grow quite quickly, enabling us to move later on from Throgmorton Avenue to swisher premises at Roman House in Fore Street, close to what is now Morgan Chase's office.

In my early days in such a small company, I was, effectively, under everybody's wing — that is, all the senior staff guided me where necessary. I felt I already understood the trade of broking very well, but it was a market based on relationships and, starting with a blank client sheet, I set about developing mine. I was given some lines of business and developed others — especially with my former employers at A&NZ. As I came with an open mind, I was able to develop my own style — which, I must say, a lot of people have copied over the years. I'd describe it as a gentle, although quick and sharp, style — persuasive, without being pushy. Summed up thus: "These are the prices, do you want to deal with me? If so, that's fine. I can give you the name of so and so ..."

In that first period S&H were largely brokers in Scandinavian currencies and one day somebody said to me it was time to "short" these currencies. (The objective of currency trading is to exchange one currency for another with the expectation that the market rate or price will change such that the currency you have bought has appreciated in value relative to the currency you have sold. If the currency you have bought appreciates in value and you close your open position by selling this currency — or effectively buying the currency that you originally sold — then you are locking in a profit. If the currency depreciates in value and you close your open position by selling this currency, or effectively buying the currency you have sold, then you are realising a loss. Buying a currency is synonymous with taking a "long" position in that currency, while selling a currency is synonymous with "shorting" that currency.)

When I enquired why he wanted to sell, he replied: "Because the ports are freezing up." "But, the ports don't freeze up these days," I informed him. "Well, don't say a word to anybody. We do a lot of business telling them this!" Such was the character of the market and many of the people I was working with.

As time went on we looked to expand into deutschmarks against sterling and applied formally to extend the scope of our currency dealings. We went into forward dollars against sterling and took on the BOLSA (Bank of London South America) account — one that we gained from their chief dealer, whom I had got to know. It was a big and difficult account and we had to be on our toes to retain it. Other key lines of business were with Lloyds Bank and Standard Chartered.

Another interesting feature of those far-off days was what would now seem like primitive communications. Take the issue of payment. Today, deals and settlement are done at the flick of a button or a computer keystroke. Not so then. In the 1950s the banks could pay for the delivery of foreign exchange settlement in one of three ways: one was by mail, air mail or telegraphic transfer via the Cable and Wireless Shop near the Stock Exchange!

We worked very hard and, as business grew, younger people, such as Val Edwards's son Brian, came in. This new generation began to take over from the older personality brokers in this changing era of highly competitive markets. Winning business from friends was no longer good enough and a new, more pro-active, approach was required, and this came from the younger brokers.

Three guys who worked at S&H were to have a particular significance for me. David Riley and Peter Doney were to become central players in the early years after the new company was formed in 1971, while Larry Woolman, who arrived at S&H not long after me, was to think long and hard about joining the new venture, before eventually deciding to stay put. Larry had been in insurance where he earned around £380 a year and joined S&H in 1960 for £400 a year. Like a lot of recruits at the time he had no idea what the money markets were and, in fact, stumbled upon foreign exchange broking when looking in the newspapers for an insurance broking job. Larry arrived soon after Peter Savage died, which left the firm being run by partners Bill Heath, Ginger Weedon and Val Edwards. Val was the newest and most junior partner and his two sons, Michael and Brian, worked alongside me in the body of the business. None of the Edwards family had worked in banking or broking before —which was to have great significance ten years down the line.

Larry started as a trainee under my wing and eventually joined the board some years later when Ginger Weedon stood down. In those days the partners used to sit at the dealing boards, which was a bit awkward because they very rarely plugged into them to do any business! Indeed, I generated the bulk of the spot business in forward marks against sterling and began to make a name for myself. Although the partners appeared to leave most of the work to Larry, the Edwards brothers and myself, I was keen to learn, happy to work hard, hungry for success and viewed these as very happy days.

The market was growing and every day was an adventure — you certainly never knew what was going to happen — which was certainly true one evening when Larry and I went out on a Black Tie evening with S&H clients; first to the Playhouse Theatre close to Charing Cross Station, followed by drinks at a club. By 3am Larry and I decided it wasn't worth going home, so we tried — unsuccessfully as it turned out — to get hotel rooms. Failing to do so, we were left with no option but to make for the office and sleep in our chairs. That was all right, except that I had a high-profile lunch with the Bank of England that day which saw me discard the dinner jacket and bowtie and dash out at the last minute to buy an ill-fitting suit. I turned up for lunch looking like a scarecrow!

If each day brought its share of uncertainties, one thing I was confident about was that the Bank of England would help brokers, like S&H, grow along with the banks, which meant that when the market became global, the City and its brokers would be at the centre. By the early 60s markets had improved and S&H had improved to the point that we began to compete with the top brokers, Marshall and Harlow Meyer. S&H were fortunate in that the explosive growth of the money markets from the early 60s was in areas in which we had expertise.

Money broking was proving to be one of the most successful forms of business in the City. In the early 60s it was every schoolboy's ambition to earn £1,000 a year by the age of 30. By contrast, even in a small company like S&H, which had more limited ambitions, the more talented brokers would have expected to earn more than that. By the same token, no one could have anticipated the kind of sums that would be made some 20 years on.

As S&H became more successful, we ploughed back our profits. We put everything into developing the company. This was fine for a while, but it has to be said that we made some poor decisions along the way and took on people at a senior level — not for their ability, but because they were friends of the partners. These recruits did not contribute to the business: a case of "jobs for the boys", I'm afraid.

I felt strongly about what was going on and, for the first time, I spoke up. And, in so doing, I sparked something of a "revolution". I told the partners: "We don't need the new boys." To which, they replied: "But these people are famous." "They might be famous," I insisted, "but they're not famous in the markets." They were being brought in for posts like Marketing Director, which did not contribute directly to the bottom line on the balance sheet. I felt that, in having to carry their large salaries and the expense accounts that came with them, our development was threatened. The problem was that "non-working" management was just too expensive. For their part, they felt that, because they were management and shareholders, they could do as they liked. Unfortunately, it doesn't work that way.

Although I lost the argument, this episode had a double outcome. For me, it merely confirmed what I had long suspected: that most of my colleagues were merely average brokers and that the S&H management could be pretty ineffective. For the bosses, it confirmed that I had talent and, above all, could be bold. In kicking up about the situation, which was a big moment for me, I had made my mark. Some time later, the management signified my "coming of age", as it were, by offering me a deal which made me a director and gave me a 26% stake in the company. This wasn't bad for a 26-year-old and, though I had misgivings about board policy and decision-making, I was very pleased at this promotion which made me feel that at last I could help drive the business forward.

The company had finally sat up and taken notice of me — a process that had taken a few years and a long and winding road to come to fruition. On that road there had been key moments when events offered me the chance to make an impact. I think I made a bit of a name for myself on that now-infamous Friday in November 1963 when President Kennedy was assassinated in Dallas.

We worked on alternate Saturday mornings in those days and so, the morning after the momentous event, all brokers were in and watching for market reaction. After assessing the situation, I said that, with the Americans typically "repatriating" their currency in times of crisis, the dollar should be bought. We had read the market correctly.

Kennedy's assassination was one of many external events to rock the markets. Another was the 1967 devaluation of sterling. Throughout the fifties and early sixties, "runs" on the pound, when it was sold heavily in the markets, had become almost a routine event; but devaluation was different. That October weekend — containing the famous Harold Wilson "the pound in your pocket wouldn't be affected" pledge — led to huge speculation in the markets. Just to add to the fun I seem to recall that, at the time, the lira was being devalued yet again — but that was almost a weekly occurrence in those days!

By the mid-60s, I was managing director of S&H and it fell to me to map out the firm's future. Despite my reservations, the firm had continued to grow throughout the sixties and we took on board the new Eurodollar products as they came along. We were quite strong operators and we discovered arbitrage possibilities that were introduced and exploited successfully. This success also saw us look at the prospect of expanding into New York.

I set out my ideas in a presentation to management in which I generally foresaw the London foreign exchange market going completely international in all forms of dealing, involving overseas branches, where possible, in our own name. Over five years I looked to new operations in the US, Switzerland, Germany, Italy, Japan and Austria. Within this "world-wide" network, I anticipated London remaining the centre of it all and opening 24 hours a day. This was an exciting plan, but it was based on careful expansion, which I saw as vital. "Rather not expand at all, than expand badly" was my motto.

Around this time, the two men who were to play a significant role in my future business life, had joined S&H. David Riley was a fellow director who transacted foreign deposit dealing, while Peter Doney had joined from retail banking and would gain vital experience working in New York. I had first met David in the sixties when he worked in traditional broking and, when he moved to S&H, it became clear there was a certain "chemistry" between us. David would eventually leave for Harlow Meyer because of S&H's emphasis which, while not precluding Euro deposit broking, had not embraced it.

David, on the other hand, was convinced the future was in Eurocurrency and became even more sure after The Economist published an article in 1969, which predicted that within ten years Europe would have a common currency. He gave a presentation on this to his new employers at Harlow Meyer and, such was the reaction, that within four days he had been switched from foreign exchange to deposits. We did not realise it then but this was a seminal moment on the road that was to lead to our forming a new company just two years later.

Eurocurrency was the next big thing and our new venture was to exploit this to the full. David would lead the way in this. He brought a lot of seemingly contradictory skills to the Eurodollar party. While highly innovative, he was also a stickler for the disciplined approach: accurate terminology was crucial to him and it changed the nature of the deposits market and his disciplines are still to be seen in the markets some 30 or more years on.

That was the future. For the time being, I still had an important role at S&H. Charged with looking at the growth possibilities, I suggested to the board that a business plan be put in place, but their response was very casual and this was the first real signal to me that it was nearly time to look elsewhere to satisfy my ambitions. Later on, the board woke up to the need for change — as when Val Edwards left the company and moved to Switzerland — but it was too little, too late.

S&H also started an operation in the United States in 1969 and I went to New York for six months to ensure that the right approach was adopted and that the business got off the ground. With hindsight, these were the wrong moments to be away from London. These were, indeed, difficult days at S&H. The firm had lost its way and things were just not working. The board's decision-making had deteriorated and there was not enough forward thinking. And when David Riley, with whom I had worked closely, upped sticks for Harlow Meyer, the writing was on the wall for me.

In the early days everything had seemed new and exciting at S&H and it was only in later years, after it had expanded, that it became apparent there was an imbalance in the business. On the one hand, there was Michael and Brian Edwards — both of whom were made associate partners, with Michael later becoming a joint managing director alongside me. Our titles were the only things we had in common. We had vastly differing personalities; my energy and enthusiasm contrasted with his general failure to be proactive. He seemed to be content to let things happen. Make no mistake about it, both the Edwards brothers were nice guys but rather passive.

This was the basis of the imbalance that many of my colleagues perceived in S&H towards the end of the sixties. They felt, that I was, quite simply, better at my job. I was regarded as the dynamo of the business and was always "go, go, go." I led the forex side at S&H and we were the income generators. Mike Edwards ran the deposit side. Forex brokers were contemptuous of the deposit brokers and I guess it came as no surprise that S&H split heavily into Tullett and Edwards camps. And, indeed, one of the reasons David Riley left was because of the nepotism that was rife in a part of the company.

With the office politics really hotting up, I did my best to try to heal the rift that had grown because I believed it was damaging our productivity and market reputation. But it was not to be and things grew worse. Larry Woolman, who was made an assistant director around this time, recalls a secret meeting, which was called with a view to demoting me from joint MD to an ordinary director.

Although this coup failed, I knew it was time for me to move on. I approached the banks and got their backing and with the market explosion that was taking place, this was an ideal time to set up a new company. The booming market created a demand for new brokers who could challenge the old establishment — the traditional "blue bloods".

Up to 1968 there was no scope for anyone to go out on their own in broking as the market was a closed shop through the Foreign Exchange Brokers Association (FEBA). In 1969 the brakes were taken off and a phenomenal growth took place. At this stage, the London brokers could operate globally subject to the approval of the overseas centres' authorities. A window of opportunity for a new company was thus opened.

As I considered my next move, a new decade had begun and the City of London was starting to look a very different place. There was a new London Bridge and work had begun on the City's first skyscraper — the NatWest Tower. Everywhere you could sense change in the air. These were exciting times and there was more ahead and I was determined to be part of it.

4

THE BREAKTHROUGH

I was never one for the orthodox way and the manner of my leaving Savage & Heath was no exception. When I resigned in 1971 I did so without telling my fellow directors. Instead, I announced my intentions through the press which carried a piece saying I was starting my own company. This shook my colleagues, created a bit of a stir in the market and raised my profile significantly.

I was confident about the future. I had gained a lot of experience and developed a growing reputation among my peers in the marketplace — as one broker described me at the time: "A small man with a big presence."

On resigning I actually considered a series of options — with offers from a number of areas. But I'd pretty well made up my mind that I was going to start my own company and I knew the people I wanted to join me. Before taking the leap I had canvassed an inner group of colleagues and associates about my idea of forming a new company, to be called "D. Tullett & Co" to trade in the money markets which, by then, was comprised of three elements: foreign exchange, domestic sterling and Eurocurrency deposits.

So, I had every reason to be optimistic about such an

enterprise. Throughout the 60s the markets had operated within something of a contradiction: while the UK economy was turbulent, with wild trade swings and industrial unrest and in apparent decline, the City was forging ahead and growing stronger as London looked to resume its position at the centre of the international financial universe. During the 60s the markets were progressively freed up and one of the fastest growers was proving to be the dollar deposit market — or the Eurodollar as it became known. Dollar deposits were earned and owned by foreigners and left in London for the short term on better rates than in the US or elsewhere.

And there was money to be made. In the early days of the Eurodollar there was a real wheeze, which Kleinwort Benson was the first to cotton on to and exploit. If you borrowed Federal funds on a Thursday to Friday you paid one day's interest. However, with these same funds lent out from Friday to Monday you could receive three day's interest. To benefit from this you had to be a member of the Federal Bank's Clearing System

By the start of the 70s the Eurodollar was central to the City's money markets. Some 80% of the Eurodollar pool was traded through London, which had become its major focus. The fact that it was as much a centre for Eurodollars as it was for sterling, was mainly down to the fact that it was able to exploit a series of natural advantages over its rivals — particularly, the City's pool of talent, its front and back office expertise and London's time zone in relation to all markets, and America in particular. This meant that London had again become the hub of international finance with the number of foreign banks operating there doubling between 1960 and 1970. US banks, especially, flooded in — with the Moorgate district becoming known as the "Avenue of the Americas".

If it was a busy time, it was also a friendly time. It was a good market to be in with pleasant people around. Take the issue of technology, a crucial factor in the years that were to follow. In those days, the only technology was the adding machine, which could handle the basic calculations of adding, subtracting, multiplication and division. In practice, though, a lot of the calculations were done manually: you could calculate by simple multiplication accurately enough to be able to say what a figure should be. Brokers and dealers helped each other with these calculations because it was in everyone's interests to get them right. The market was growing faster than any of us could handle on our own and there was more than enough business to go around.

But if it was a happy environment, it was also a rather narrow one. It was almost exclusively a male world and we were some way off the broader social make-up that would follow. There may have been half a dozen women among all the brokers. In fact, we had a very good female broker at S&H who worked on Eurodollars, but the dealers were uncomfortable with it because they thought that a woman handling an account might get business through other means. Indeed, Anita, who became my second wife, had seen the male-dominated environment from the vantage point of the back office at S&H where she worked on contracts. She witnessed a culture of heavy drinking and strong language and recalls how on Fridays things could get, what she called, "a little personal".

From the outset, broking had also been an industry populated in the main by former public schoolboys — so producing an insular world where you couldn't get a job in a broking house unless you had the "inside track" of knowing someone there. Hitherto, it had not been a place for women or those educated outside the private sector with the "old school tie" system generating dealers and brokers with maverick attitudes. But this was to change dramatically. More people with qualifications were coming through, however, and they were showing the market a new way to both deal and to behave. It was a time of great change, probably one of the biggest upheavals since the markets re-opened in 1951 following the wartime hibernation. A new order was taking shape.

This was the City as we entered the 70s. To a large extent it was part of the general social change taking place in Britain in the 60s: a lot of people were working hard and trying to make their way in the world. The market was made up of the sons of those who had been through tough times in the war and those wanting to learn the intricacies of how things move and why things happen. It was a great mix which created an exciting time.

Against this backdrop I planned to launch my business. It was obvious that any new venture would have to get to grips with Eurodollar dealing and this was not my strong suit. I discussed this with Peter Doney, who was keen to join a new set-up, and, understandably, his biggest concern was that the market we both knew — in forwards and, to a limited degree, the spot market — would be too limited for a new company, which would make us vulnerable as a result.

Peter felt that spot and forward dollar sterling and the mark etc were far too small an area of the overall market in which to specialise. We had to get into Eurodollars — the hot market. For his part, David Riley had helped pioneer this market and was doing very well in this section of Harlow Meyer. David was an astute man and a totally free spirit — a real one-off. He was 6ft 2in, wore a beard and sandals and enjoyed free-fall wrestling (out of the office, I might say). But, more importantly, he really knew his business.

It was agreed that Peter would approach him about joining our venture. It turned out that David was happy to link up but wanted a significant say in the company. After some discussion, during which it was agreed that Eurocurrency would be the company's initial driving force and earning power, the deal was done and Tullett & Riley was born. I know that Peter always felt the company could not have happened without David's Eurodollar skills. He believed that, without David, we might have traded successfully in spot and forward dollar sterling, but that this would not have allowed us to recruit staff and so expand. While David's influence cannot be understated, it's difficult to say for sure what the outcome would have been without him. A fourth member of the founding team was Colin Probets who was another of the personality brokers. Colin was a real tough guy — he had played rugby and been a boxer in his time — but, like so many in our business, found it difficult to keep fit. Sadly, Colin died in 2003.

Richard Magee joined the company at the outset and was to be with the company for 25 years, during which time he built a career that eventually saw him rise to the top. As I mentioned earlier, one other who was party to the original plans to form the company was Larry Woolman, but he eventually decided not to get on the bus. I wonder if he ever felt like Pete Best, the "fifth Beatle", who left the group before it became famous.

In the new set up, which was formally announced to the market in June 1971, David and I, as joint managing directors, would both have a 25% share with Peter holding an 18% stake; the balance was split between the rest of the staff. We each brought a variety of expertise to the business: I brought my experience of the foreign exchange markets, David would spearhead our attack on Eurocurrency and Peter, a fine mathematician, would specialise in technology, a deployment which was to prove vital to us.

As we geared up for the off, what kind of reception did we anticipate? I think it's true to say that the markets didn't feel the need for another broker; after all, big houses, such as Marshall and Harlow Meyer, were dominating the scene. As the new kids on the block, a number of FEBA restrictions were put in our way. To apply for a foreign exchange trading licence we needed the sponsorship of four major banks. Having obtained this sponsorship we were made to wait a long time for our application to be processed. In addition, we had to agree, initially, to a FEBA condition not to recruit staff from existing brokers.

One way or another, our arrival in the market had caused a good deal of controversy within FEBA — and it was all too easy to conclude that the restrictions placed in our way was an act of sour grapes on the part of the broking "establishment". But we always believed that, with a number of upheavals taking place then, there was scope for a small, but innovative, company to come in and take on the "old guard". We were sure we could bring a dynamism to the market.

So, we began life in August 1971 at 38, Cannon Street, above Mansion House Underground station and on our first day we earned £1,000 brokerage — largely made up of a one-year Eurodeposit deal for Bank of America and Standard Chartered (two of our sponsors). Later, as we celebrated at a nearby pub, I recall saying: "Well, that's the first month's rent paid!" Within six months we were making £3,000 to £4,000 a day and soon, with about 20 staff on board, £10,000 a day became typical. Things were going well.

We soon realised, however, that we had to make alterations to our premises if we were to make the most of our ideas. The original team of 12 at 38 Cannon Street wanted to develop the offices to meet our changing needs. We particularly wanted to open up what had previously been two offices to create one dealing room. We eventually achieved this, but it was not without its dramas. One day during the refurbishment, a builder came along with his hammer and loosened a load of bricks which fell into the office below narrowly missing an unsuspecting employee sitting there!

With our offices sorted out we continued on our heady, at times breathless, journey across new frontiers in the markets. While Euro currencies were booming, we waited patiently for our forex licence. I was aware that, in undertaking this project, it would be a painstaking business — but the licence would benefit us enormously in the long term. In the short term, a lot of diplomacy would be needed by me as I set about my task. And even though we were made to wait, I simply kept my cool and stayed in touch with all my potential clients ready for the off.

Meanwhile, we had a living to make. Quickly accepting that a new company could not afford to end up as a small player in a big market, we aimed at becoming a big player! To achieve this, we reinforced the Eurodollar section, which had started with a team of four. With this market booming we switched most of our resources to it. We couldn't sit still: so, while we waited for our licence, we very successfully got stuck into Eurodollar broking. For the time being, the Eurodollar was the only show in town for us.

We felt we could succeed through innovation and sharp elbows. From the start we went about things in an entirely different way from the traditional London broking houses. In those days the market, purely by habit, opened at 8.30am and virtually closed down between 12.30 and 2.30pm for a long lunch, and finished at 5pm. David and I agreed some unprecedented hours of business: our staff would be in at 7.30am as we wanted the world to see our lights showing in our offices: with lunch cancelled, we found we transacted good business between 12.30 and 2.30pm!

Our final touch was to stay open until 6pm. But the day didn't end there. Well into the night, we interviewed potential recruits. When Tullett & Riley was being set up, the FEBA restriction meant we were not allowed to poach staff from within the industry, but agreed, instead, to recruit from outside.

Wrapped up in our daily concerns, particularly bringing in the money, and given the recruitment limits that had been set for us, we only had limited time to think ahead with such issues as extra staff. To begin with, we gambled on recruiting enthusiastic novices from outside the business who had the right qualities and who showed promise. We were expanding quickly, we needed staff quickly — so we took a few chances and, generally speaking, it worked out.

Another innovation was the introduction of an in-house training scheme, which had the support of the banks. This was the first practical training of its kind on the broker side of the business. An early recruit was Alan Styant, who was to go a long way with the company.

Alan had spent five years in Monte Carlo working for the shipping magnate Stavros Niarchos and, while there, took a course which led to his becoming a Company Secretary. After qualifying, he returned to London with Niarchos, but it wasn't working out. Part of his duties involved managing the Niarchos portfolio and he handled foreign exchange and shares and also became familiar with the gold and silver markets.

Having this background, it was suggested he moved into money broking, which was beginning to boom. So, he was introduced to Tulletts through a headhunter and had an interview with me. This took place very early one morning and lasted about 3-4 minutes, during which time I asked him a few basic questions and, confident he could do a job for us, then said: "When can you start?" It was agreed Alan would start a couple of months later.

So, at 29, he joined the company, knowing nothing about money broking and no doubt wondering what he'd let himself in for. Alan sat with me on the foreign exchange (or forex) desk working on forward sterling. In various spells I guess Alan spent 10 of the next 25 years working next to me. He found the markets bemusing to begin with. A lot of shouting and screaming with appalling language at times. And the job was a great leveler: his age and previous seniority at Niarchos counted for nothing with us and he was treated like the new boy who got the sandwiches! It was a shock to his system, but after a few months he was given the chance to handle his own accounts and got to enjoy the work, the people and the life that went with the job. Alan came to appreciate what I had said at his interview: "We like to work hard and play hard!"

Another key appointment was David Lowe as our Company Secretary. David had worked in the financial sector in London doing the occasional deal in the money markets. In the summer of 1972 he answered our advertisement in the national press and so began a near 25-year association with Tulletts. He may have had a grand title, but in those early days David did everything from compiling the consolidated accounts to ensuring the toilets were unblocked! As he once boasted: "Anything that wasn't broking at Tullett & Riley, was me!"

David must have got an inkling of what life with me and money broking would be like when, some four weeks after he joined, I breezed into the office to a pre-arranged meeting with him, and roundly proclaimed before disappearing with similar speed: "There's just two things you need to know: you can charge anything you like to expenses; and you must make sure the brokers are back from lunch by 2.30pm!"

So, we had got off to a good start and, although business was moving forward, we had to watch our cashflow carefully. We certainly got to know the tricks of the trade when it came to clients delaying payment. For example, when you rang a client's accounts department, you would often be greeted with: "I can't understand any delay, the cheque's definitely in the post!" Another client delaying tactic would be to query an invoice and suggest you look into it. "Next week, will be fine," they would reply, quickly followed by the phone being put down.

At that early stage, Tullett & Riley were seventh in the league of eight brokers and weren't attracting enough liquidity. So we had to beg, steal or borrow favours from the banks to allow us to give them a price or work on an order. Alan Styant took six months to feel reasonably comfortable with the markets and became popular with colleagues and clients alike. He started on "spot" — which was simple, as you are working with just two numbers — and moved on to "forwards" which is more complex.

I liked to think that, in the early days, the fact that I was one of the best-known forwards brokers in the industry was clearly an asset to us. I kicked-off most things as it took most of the rest of the team some while to build up relationships. Before too long, the team, which I set up and coached, began to attract some good liquidity and we moved up the league table quickly.

My office style took few prisoners. Inevitably, I was totally focused on the job: in office hours you talked to your clients constantly, there would be no let-up — no coffee breaks or stopping to read the newspaper. Alan Styant thought my expressions summed up my approach at the time. Apparently, if told: "There's nothing going on", I would reply: "There's always something going on!" Or I might exhort my team to phone our clients by saying to them: "Come on, round the rink!" – which meant calling each of their batch of 10 banks, and doing this over and over again by finding something to say and try to get an order out of them. Or my favourite piece of encouragement: "When they're talking to you, they can't be talking to anyone else!" I could also try to catch my team out with off-the-cuff enquiries like: "What's your seven-and-a-half months?" as they struggled to check what it was.

But one thing colleagues noticed particularly about my approach, and I know it intrigued some, was that in any argument in the office I rarely, if ever, sought the last word. In the midst of a flare-up with a colleague, however junior, once I had made my point I would get on with my work, ignoring any fuss that carried on around me.

All this could be quite intimidating, but stimulating and great fun as well. And once the day was over it was into the bar for drinks and a bit of bonding. In addition, every newcomer had dinner at my home at least once — and not every boss did that. I accept that I was forceful in the office, but hope that I was also inspiring and that, along with bringing in good directors from outside, this helped build Tulletts.

Here we were then, the new guys doing things differently and, within a few months, we were racing ahead. Tullett & Riley moved forward with a fair bit of panache and we broke our business targets on a daily basis. We matched the unusual way we organised ourselves with an innovative approach to the marketplace itself.

We may have been the newcomers, but we showed we knew how to make money through some innovative ideas in the market that did exceptionally well. We made a lot of money and this enabled us to offer good salaries in an attempt to recruit good staff. Almost from the beginning, the market had taken us seriously and, far from being seen as an up-start company, we were viewed positively and regarded as a competitor who would not fade away.

It was hard work. But life wasn't without its light-hearted, sometimes hilarious, moments. One came when Colin Probets, forever the office joker, accidentally fired off a sporting gun in the office and narrowly missed hitting David Riley! Another came a few months in when we all went out on our first Christmas party just four months or so after we launched. The evening started out at a bistro just off Fleet Street, but we soon discovered it had no drinks licence. So we decided to move into the West End: but how we were going to get there? One of our number went out into Fleet Street and spotted a line of newspaper vans and with commendable ingenuity bribed one of the drivers to let us pile into the back and off we went. Dirty and uncomfortable it may have been, but we were where we wanted to be — typical of our unconventional approach to things!

All along we knew that to make our mark we had to do things differently at Tullett & Riley and so developed ideas on the Eurocurrency side designed to get banks to sit up and take note of us. The banks could not understand how we could do our deals and make so much money. The key to this was a "little secret" we developed and which enabled us to create deals the banks thought impossible.

As a result, we commanded respect and our growing reputation helped us to forge important links with the banks. Eventually, though, the market discovered our "secret" and copied it.

We had opened to what seemed a frenzy of money-making. Side by side with this, I continued to lobby for our foreign exchange licence. I think the market, to some extent, could not understand why we bothered. After all, we were making plenty of money through Eurodollars and foreign exchange was not that lucrative, anyway. But it was partly a prestige thing. It was a badge of acceptability, which, in the long run, I still felt we needed.

Equally, we needed a foreign exchange outlet to show the market we were a multi-product company and not simply boutique brokers. And, although this side of the business was not as profitable as Eurodollars, it was vital to our long-term survival, so that when, some years later, the market returned to foreign exchange — although not to the detriment of the other markets — we were well placed to take advantage.

Our difficulty in getting a licence for foreign exchange

dealing was rooted in market history. After 1945 dealing was regulated by a pact between the Foreign Exchange Committee, which looked after the banks, and the Foreign Exchange Brokers Association, which handled brokers' interests. The banks passed all the foreign exchange dealing with other banks through the association's then nine members, while the brokers agreed not to deal directly with commercial clients.

As Tullett & Riley arrived on the scene in the early 70s, consolidation among the largest brokers in London was well under way and with many niche companies starting up, regulations would eventually change to the extent that these days you don't need to be a member of FEBA (now the Wholesale Markets Brokers' Association) to be a broker. But in those days you did and so, for over a year, we tried in vain to become an association member and so gain a licence. Eventually, the Bank of England intervened and put pressure on the Foreign Exchange Committee pointing out that, as we had the proper number of proposers, we should be granted the licence without further delay. Our frustration was about to end.

After the licence came through, I launched our foreign exchange operation in June 1972, just a month after Union Discount beat us to the title of first new forex broker since the war. It's true to say that though the forex market was largely domestic and marginally profitable, we believed it would internationalise. And anyway, in the short term, it enabled us to establish our links with the banks and get in our direct lines of business to clients on all products.

And as a footnote to this episode, I should add that after the licence was granted a bizarre situation developed. For, having originally been seen as a renegade who had fought them, the brokers' committee was to later ask me to join them. A case of "poacher turned gamekeeper" perhaps?

Now we were firing on all cylinders. Whichever area of the

business we worked in, we were creating new work practices to cope with an operating environment few, if any, of us had been used to. Peter, for instance, was on the telephone all the time chasing his US contacts, and in the first few years he flew to America quite a bit. A typical working weekend for him would comprise flying to the US on a Friday afternoon; conducting business, followed by lunch and dinner on Saturday; flying back to Britain on Sunday; and reporting back to the office Monday morning. Quite a schedule!

My partners were travelling the world in an attempt to meet people and drum up business. We were, in short, buzzing. A team of different temperaments and talents coming together and creating success — largely because, though we didn't always agree about everything, we listened to each other and arrived at decisions democratically. The critical thing was that everyone had their say and as individuals we trusted each other implicitly. Regardless of our views on a subject, once we took the decision to do something, we all got behind it.

With such unity and drive we soon became market leaders by getting the better of the older, established players who could not understand how we did it. Tullett & Riley became a market force as we moved faster than our rivals into new products and began dealing with people who, 18 months before, wouldn't have given us much chance of surviving.

From the start we had a five-year plan — but it wasn't the usual plan containing detailed targets and costings. Instead, it was based on taking a fresh look at each year's figures and modifying the operation in the light of circumstances. This enabled us to forge ahead with the occasional pause for consolidation, such as our later takeover of Nolton, the sterling brokers, which gave the company a balance to its business.

A couple of other companies started up in competition with us, but they were not risk takers like us. Essentially, we were the brokers who had come from nowhere and achieved parity with the established firms. We had taken the market by storm by taking risks not only in the way we ran the business, but also in career terms. For a start, I took a risk in contemplating the whole project; David was foregoing a senior role at Harlow Meyer; while Peter believed that he was young and energetic enough to take a gamble.

And, make no mistake, exciting though they were, the early years were not without their difficulties. Having second mortgages was worrying, but we struggled through and it was only when I was able to sell my 26% stake in Savage & Heath that we had sufficient funds to drive the business forward.

Risk taking in our day-to-day business decision-making — in what David and Peter saw as an SAS "Who Dares Wins" approach – came naturally to us. Up to the late 1960s broker recruitment was largely limited to former public school boys. From then on, state school boys began to make more of an impact — even so, by the early 1970s the market was still staid enough for Tullett & Riley to move in. The embryonic T&R team, which had started to assemble in the Savage & Heath days, was made up of sharp-witted, highly motivated, very energetic, market savvy, state-educated lads who were to dominate market proceedings from then on.

Tullett & Riley was taking on the market and its old protocols and as the market changed in the late 70s and early 80s, we were in a prime position, having embraced change ahead of our competitors. Looking back we were in the right place, at the right time, with the right attitude. And given that you are lucky if one in five business ideas can be turned into a money earner, our innovations were certainly paying rich dividends.

In the early 70s, most firms in the market, such as Marshall, Harlow Meyer and Guy Butler, were subsidiaries of large discount houses. We had no such ties, which brought many advantages. It meant that we made our decisions quickly and independently and from the beginning we decided we were more interested in long-term gains than short-term returns. So that when broker commissions became negotiable in the 80s — having previously been set by the Foreign Exchange Brokers Association — we, unlike some of our bigger competitors, went for modest fees in an attempt to build market share, as opposed to bottom-line profit. In the same way, Tullett & Riley paid no dividends in the first 10 years: apart from capital needed for such things as salaries, we ploughed all earnings back into the company.

Increasingly, our clients could see that what we may have lacked in the width of our service, we more than made up for in effort. For, in a market in which long shifts were the norm, we worked exceptionally long hours to get the business truly launched. Indeed, in those early days I was up at dawn and commuting from Kent in what was a pretty fixed routine: same time, same station, same train and same faces. For me, those journeys and City offices were somehow synonymous with cigarettes. As I didn't smoke, I used to squeeze into a non-smoking carriage that none of my smoker friends would go into. Almost everywhere you went smoke impregnated your body — so much so, that every day I had my suits cleaned and I used to wash my hair and clean my teeth all the time to fight off the smell of tobacco. It's hard to believe now that smoking was so prevalent then.

But that daily routine was about to change. By 1973 we were making serious money in London and had also started forex broking which, although not the premier market and not a great earner, was useful to us. To reinforce all this, we decided to look to the United States and became the first British money brokers into New York in our own name. While our rivals went into North America via Toronto, we took on the US directly, believing we could change the attitude of the US banks. This was a very significant moment and it proved to be one of the best decisions we made.

Arriving in New York, I couldn't help but think about an earlier episode in the "Big Apple" when I worked for Savage & Heath. We were looking at three companies to possibly get involved with and having seen all the candidates we made a decision and then I had the task of letting the unsuccessful firms know. So, I walked into this senior broker's office and said: "Well, I'll come straight to the point, I don't want to waste your time. Thank you very much for the time you've spent with us, we don't think it's the best fit for us and we're going along with another company." Pushing his jacket to one side and revealing a large handgun, he replied: "Well, I'm pretty upset about that!" I feared for my life. He was certainly upset — but, luckily, as it turned out, not enough to shoot me!

The reason I went to New York was that, having worked there in 1969 and 1970, I had existing friends and contacts to call upon. As I settled in, this second time around, I found that, with UK exchange controls in place — and prior to gaining UK permission for more funds — we were trying to start an operation limited to spending just £30 a day. Fortunately, enough money came through in time to pay the hotel bill, otherwise the Hilton would have thrown us out into the street. Eventually, I rented a house in New Jersey and commuted to work each day: it was far less expensive.

Another stroke of luck came when a business friend gave me one of his company's attics to use as an office, with the added advantage of having the prestigious address of No 1 Wall Street. The understanding was that we would pay him rent when we could afford it. In turn, I started to recruit people in New York and even though I had to tell them I did not know what I could pay them, there was enough trust around and it all worked well.

These were great days. Fun days. But they were days packed with hard work and total trust in the judgment and decision-making of everybody in the company. New York was also an early example of our declared policy of trying, where we could, to open our own offices and avoid local partnerships. Our rivals, in turn, opted for Toronto in Canada as a centre from which to operate into the US.

But New York proved the right choice in so many ways. This was chiefly because, unlike our competitors, we spotted something crucial about Eurodollars: the other inter-North American markets were open to us. Though they could not be held physically in New York, Eurodollars could be traded there because the market decisions were being taken by the New York headquarters of big US banks such as Chase Manhattan and JP Morgan. We saw that banks didn't need to deal with brokers in Toronto, when they could deal with us in New York — even if the order, and subsequently the funds, was placed through London or Nassau. We checked with the Federal Reserve and they said they could see no reason why we couldn't trade in this way — particularly as New York was not a market they regulated. So, when we opened in New York, we used this "loophole" and took the market to the banks that, to our great delight, dropped their dealings with other brokers and switched to us.

Meanwhile, our rivals tried to compete with us long distance. To counter this and consolidate our position, we linked up with Paul Matthews, another of my former Savage & Heath colleagues, who was based in New York. Later on, Peter and Colin took it in turn to have spells in the Wall Street office.

The success of New York saw us expand and, over a period of four years, we opened a series of strategic offices around the world — either full branches or set up with associates — which enabled us to compete with our rivals on a level playing field. New York was followed from 1978 to 1985 by the opening of offices in Hong Kong, Singapore, Abu Dhabi (later replaced by Bahrain), Toronto, Belgium, Frankfurt, Luxemburg and Australia.

The Middle East had been of particular interest to us. To investigate the possibility, Alan Styant, Peter Doney and I flew to Abu Dhabi — the first of many eventful trips which were always full of incident. To begin with, the flight was late and arrived at about 3am local time. The three of us were dishevelled and extremely tired and, to make matters worse, scenes at the airport were chaotic and we were told that there were no hotels available in town.

However, I had a word in a British Airways ear and, after I muttered the magic words that "it didn't matter how much it cost", we were fixed up with a "suite" in the Zacca Hotel. While that sounded fine, the good news ended there. The Zacca turned out to be a dive in a side street. Shown to our rooms, we found that the air conditioning was hanging off the wall, the curtains were practically on the floor and there were two single beds and a camp bed. Peter drew the short straw and had the camp bed which when he went to sleep on it folded up and shot back up into the wall! As soon as we could, we abandoned our flea-ridden beds and moved hotels

I also recall another incident towards the end of a later trip to Abu Dhabi. Our team arrived at the airport to discover chaos and confusion in the wake of a failed assassination attempt on a senior government minister. At first we couldn't get out of the airport, but finally I got on a Europe-bound plane as I headed for Switzerland.

David Lowe, on the other hand, struggling to find a flight to Singapore and fearing being stranded, decided to get on the next plane out and so settled for India, instead. After a day or so, the office in London became quite concerned at his whereabouts only to discover he had booked into a luxury hotel in Bombay and was generally enjoying life awaiting a connection to Singapore!

On yet another trip to Abu Dhabi, David Riley, having booked into a hotel for three nights, found the hotel management demanding payment every day with each successive bill rising by 30%. We were new to the scene and having to learn fast!

I also remember a fish restaurant there which had a board outside saying: "Catch of the Day" with a space left for whatever fish was available. Passing by one morning we noticed someone had written underneath "Catch of the Day" the word "typhoid"!

Once the decision had been made to open in Abu Dhabi in 1978, Anita and our sons, Jonathan and Kevin — during their school vacation — joined me on a business trip there to help set up shop. Again, it was not without its moments. On our way to the business meeting our Avis hire car blew up on a desert road. We left the car there and drove to the meeting in a pick-up truck which had noisy, smelly goats on the back. To the consternation of the others, I took the best seat, as I needed to be as fresh as possible to conduct the meeting.

Our venture into Abu Dhabi was particularly interesting. We wanted to see if we could gain a toehold among the oil states and we liked the look of Abu Dhabi because it was the commercial centre; it was an "oil" economy; it was a reasonable place for UK expatriates to live and work; and we had a good relationship with its Currency Board, part of its central bank. We had been scouring the Middle East with a view to plugging into the Petrodollars market and, after a fair bit of preparatory work by me in 1976-77, we gained the licence and Alan Styant became the first manager there. Alan and myself and our respective families got the show on the road in Abu Dhabi. We worked hard as a team and made a good name for ourselves. Overall, the move was a success, although we never got our hands on the Petrodollars, which seemed to go straight to London. We moved out of Abu Dhabi in 1980 and set up in Bahrain, where Alan again negotiated the licence.

The Middle East proved a successful area for us and, as well as Abu Dhabi, we also moved into Bahrain, Kuwait and the Lebanon — the latter being a really tough assignment in the midst of political turmoil and which saw our staff working in bullet-riddled offices that were protected by sandbags!

Tullett's international strategy was based on the feeling that we needed to be in every market we possibly could — even if we were only second, third or fourth shout on an order and the market, overall, was something of a loss leader. We were sure that these markets would inter-link at some point. And, of course, we were right: they did and our strategy paid off. Though accumulating a bigger share of the market was difficult, because our competitors had taken on partners with long-established contacts, we proved faster on our feet and when the markets began to move we found ways to link them, resulting in good profitability.

Our success was reflected in the growing size of the company. Having started with around a dozen staff — including only four seniors — by the end of the first year we were up to 50. And the numbers grew quickly from there to a high point in the 1980s when we employed 900 staff worldwide. An important feature of those years was our ability to recruit the right staff and train them to high standards — so ensuring we maintained our early business momentum.

In marked contrast to today, there were no formal training programmes to become a money broker. The dealers in the banks had training schemes, but we did not; so we set up our own in-house programme and the banks, somewhat informally, helped us to develop them. I suppose they could see that this all added to the greater professionalism of the markets.

As we were restricted in our recruitment in those early days, we had to find ways of widening the gene pool of talent available to us. Our first recruits were located via the jobs pages of the quality press and included ship's officers and ship's telegraphists.

We could see that these men, while lacking any City experience, had the right outlook and temperament and could be trained in the ways of the markets. They simply had to show that they were honest and ethical. Indeed, broking was all about quality of service.

Of course, when we were free to, we hired experienced brokers – none more so than Les Brock who, with his eventual wife Jill, would become company stalwarts and long-time friends. In his first spell, Les worked on foreign exchange and, after a period away from Tulletts, rejoined in the late 80s to spearhead our personnel side. But it was such things as the introduction of training which further enhanced our reputation, which we added to in other ways. Simple, everyday innovations and new routines went a long way to impressing the market.

When we launched there were 400 banks or licensed deposit takers operating in London and we had to work hard to get dealing relationships with some of them. By 1974, when foreign exchange dealing went international, we could say, with every confidence, that we had established ourselves in London, with New York and corresponding relationships with a number of overseas brokers.

How was it all coming together in the day-to-day life of the business? I brought all my experience to the dealing room and soon we operated by doing things "the Tullett way". Although essentially prescriptive, it was based on a mutual respect between my staff and me. I worked the brokers hard but would never ask them to do anything I was not prepared to have a go at myself. If anybody had any problems with this and continued to question its wisdom, I merely referred them to what it said at the entrance, "The name's on the door!" I reminded them, with tongue in cheek.

As an induction, all new brokers sat with me on the foreign exchange desk so that we could get to know each other. Les Brock has kindly described his spell there as "the best broking days of my life". In addition, brokers who were struggling also joined me in an attempt to revive their flagging fortunes. Some did, some didn't.

Another feature of dealing room life was my little silver bell, rung every time the sections made £1,000. At 4pm every day I would stand up and enquire around the various desks how they had fared and they would reply: "£1,000" "£2,000" and so on and with the bell ring to announce this, it introduced an element of good-natured but useful team rivalry. One day at the close of trading I asked my usual question, to be told: "Five dings, Del!" "Don't call me Del," I insisted. "And, what's five dings?" "Well, £5,000," I was informed. "Five rings of the bell!" Thereafter, £1,000 worth of business became "a ding" and (though not to my face) I became "Del".

Les Brock also recalls some hectic moments in the dealing room. For incoming and outgoing calls to clients we had a system of buttons which lit up when lines were busy. Apparently, if I was busy on one line and an incoming call came through from another client, I would gesture to other brokers to take the call. If they failed to do so, I would unplug their call and plug in mine. As Les says: "One minute you'd be speaking to your client, the next minute you'd be talking to Derek's!"

Our offices appeared at times to be held together by wires running throughout the building which formed the communications link with our clients and our markets at home and abroad. If a line went down, particularly to a key client, then it was vital to get it sorted and quick.

In such a fast-moving business, one of the crucial things was your rates and the ability to quote them instantly. I expected all my brokers to have an up-to-the-minute grasp of their rates for 1, 2, 3, 6 and 12 months, even if they could not quote them as rapidly as I could. For this I was known as "Machine-gun Tullett" and when one of my brokers queried that I was quoting too fast for dealers to understand, I was able to assure him: "Yes, but they come back and ask, don't they!"

With such hard work in the dealing room, the need to relax and let off steam was inevitable and lunchtime drinking was the stuff of legend. In the very early days, Tullett & Riley management were renowned for long lunches with clients, aimed at winning or retaining business. Some would return from a heavy session for an afternoon of hitting the dealing boards big time. With any inhibitions gone, and in a strange and somewhat dangerous state of being "drunk but not incapable", they would proceed to tear apart the currency deposit market.

After a while I had to tighten up on the lunches and its associated problem of time-keeping and punctuality. I took all this seriously because, at all costs, we had to be professional. We decided to cut back and so, instead of going to lunch and disappearing for the rest of the day, a 2.30pm deadline was set for management and brokers to return to their boards. When a core continued to ignore this I decided to act. At 2.30pm one afternoon, I instructed the security officer to change the code on the dealing room keypad and waited for the lunchtime stragglers to return. They were greeted and invited to a pep talk in my room — during which they were docked half a day's pay. Naturally, they never offended again.

But the company was going well and one of the keys to our success was the value we placed on information technology, very much in its infancy then. In Peter Doney, we had someone who could see its potential, where it would take the markets and what we needed to do with it on a day-to-day basis to gain that vital business edge. As our "technologymeister", Peter ensured we were ahead of our time. For example, he got to grips early on with the new Hewlett Packard calculators and developed some programming so that our staff could use them. It was expensive to do, but such things gave instant quotes based on facts and figures and provided us with that vital competitive edge.

At the same time we were one of the first companies to run cables into New York and then split them off. Using one line across the Atlantic, and via multiplexes on each end, we could make long-distance telephone calls to ten different offices in New York. In addition, we developed computers for our back office in London along with our own checking systems. All in all, we used Peter's IT expertise to push the technology as far as we could to make us quicker and better than our rivals, without incurring the heavy costs associated with large software houses.

But no operation, however successful, is without its setbacks. And, inevitably, we had our share in those early years. Perversely, we went too fast with some aspects of technology. Very early on we put loudspeakers into all our clients so that they could hear the prices. At that moment, it was a huge innovation in the markets; but we brought it to a halt because some clients feared a lack of confidentiality. That was disappointing, because once a deal is done, it's done. It's for everybody in the market to know within seconds. I guess we were just too far ahead of our time.

One of our biggest errors was placing too much faith at one stage in the domestic sterling market. In 1974 we took what proved a step too far by bringing in two brokers who were recommended us to run Tullett & Riley Sterling. We were not strong enough, the new brokers were not good enough and the whole episode was a disaster. The real problem was timing. Four or five years later when market conditions were right, we had another run at it. For now, though, we took the painful decision to pull out of the market — better to be out of the market completely than performing poorly in it.

The sterling market episode, while revealing an obvious weakness, also showed, perversely, one of our strengths. The partners had been able to act as a team and move quickly to take a tricky and important decision. By this time, I was a high-profile figure in the market, David had become well-known and Peter had fast-tracked himself into a maturity which gave him a growing voice. Age and seniority were not factors: the ability to get things right was. We were a fusion of individual talents and skills which brought a democracy to our decision-making. We trusted each other enough to swallow any boardroom disagreements and to say: "Let's give it a whirl!" Indeed, the outside world saw us as a focused unit — which was, in many ways, the secret of our success.

After spearheading our Middle Eastern drive, Alan Styant came back to London in late 1978 and to the forward sterling market and by then we had a superb team and were No 1 in the market. But the team was about to break up. Mike Rowley (who died recently), a former chief dealer with the Franklin National Bank, went out to New York. Shortly after, I left the desk to concentrate on the overall management of the business. Alan took over running forward sterling and later ran foreign exchange in London and eventually worldwide.

Throughout the 1970s the Tullett & Riley board remained very stable. The first change came in 1975 when the founding partners — myself, David Riley, Peter Doney and Colin Probets — were joined by Mike Everett. A further four years were to go by before the next board appointment and that saw the arrival of Mike Rowley.

Despite the obvious progress, and though we didn't know it, we were nearing the end of a momentous opening era for the company. On the deposits side, we had taken over a couple of established sterling brokers — Nolton Money and London & Westminster— which widened our expertise and proved the cornerstone of our future expansion. With me still looking after foreign exchange, Peter took over the day-to-day running of the deposits side and David went on the road with Brian Fitch, outgoing managing director of London & Westminster, which had built a business as brokers to the local authorities. David and Brian toured the UK for 12 months talking business to council treasurers.

We were about to say goodbye to the 70s — a decade in which we had set up the company and seen it grow. I was proud of our achievements done in my name and all seemed well as we entered the 80s, the rock and roll years in the City. But the early 80s would see significant changes in the running of our business and the break-up of the original team.

5

THE GROWTH

As we entered the 1980s things looked good with Tullett & Riley. In 1980 the company became Tullett & Riley International and, as well as London and New York, we were operating in Singapore, Beirut, Bahrain, Brussels, Sydney, Dusseldorf, Toronto, Abu Dhabi, Hong Kong, Los Angeles, Kuwait, Dublin and Vienna.

The "loudspeakers" episode, while bringing some cost savings in terms of human resource, was an experiment, which had proved expensive and didn't bring the returns hoped for. So, though we backed off this idea for the time being, we continued to innovate and push forward generally.

But before too long, a dark cloud was to gather over the company, which would subject us to our first real test. It was obvious to his colleagues that David Riley had been growing restless. For some time, he had had a vision of the growing Tullett & Riley group as a "financial supermarket" offering a wide variety of quality products backed up by quality service. By 1982, while he certainly felt the company had come a long way down that road and that we had laid the firm foundations for this, he saw no immediate prospect of taking this further.

He took what was, for him, the really difficult decision to

leave. Although David enjoyed the City, the company and his colleagues, he didn't feel everybody shared his "supermarket" vision and, so, he thought it was time to go. And, with his children growing up, he wanted to step back a bit and spend more time with his family. Recalling this moment, David later said to me: "To some extent, I was out of my time slot. If I'd been 10 years younger, I might have stayed 10 years longer."

David's going marked a real watershed in the company's affairs: he had been there from the outset and we would miss his influence. He had been a dynamic force and helped forge our view of where we wanted to go. It's fair to say that his vision of a supermarket was there from day one and he quit partly because our progress towards it was not quick enough for him. The irony is that the company not only became a supermarket, it eventually grew into a hypermarket.

In the 1970s the company's democratic principle had worked well. The directors had all learned a lot from each other, there had been no disagreement about the direction of the company and we had been successful. In the early years we didn't look up much — we just got on with making our business successful.

In the 1980s we were to become the victims of that success. There was far less boardroom harmony about the way forward and, in fact, there were clear differences on where we went next. The 1980s contrasted with the 70s in that the tightly-knit team became bigger and with it a broader board that brought with it the inevitable personality clashes, power struggles and rifts. Mike Everett had been on the board for several years but, with David Riley's departure, he became a more powerful figure in the company.

By 1980 we were growing at a very fast rate. But we had to take time to come up for air and think about the future. It is necessary to protect your earnings base and, if you don't think far enough ahead, then the rest of the world will overtake you. David had pushed for non-executive directors coming into the company bringing different business acumen. This brought a greater democracy because we had more directors with different ideas.

At the time of David's departure we were looking to expand. On the one hand we were discussing a possible link-up with Tokyo Forex, the leading forex broker in Japan, while on the other we sold shares to Postel, which managed the Post Office Pension Fund and was a client of ours. We were now starting to be serious players. We already had offices in New York and the Middle and Far East and suddenly in 1983 we found ourselves having to deploy staff to Tokyo to manage our new "share exchange merger" there as Tullett & Riley had a share exchange with Tokyo Forex and, acknowledging the liaison, renamed the company Tullett and Tokyo Forex.

It was around this time that Jill Brock, Les's wife, joined the company and, after various posts, succeeded Pat Sach as my secretary. Jill was highly efficient, intelligent and a fun person to have alongside and Jill contributed greatly to what she rightly described as the "family atmosphere" at Tulletts. I valued her input enormously down the years — not least her opinions on subjects, which often gave me another angle from which to view things.

I know it isn't easy for executive secretaries, but Jill always managed to cope. As a CEO, I know my hectic life could be difficult to keep pace with. Like the day I rushed into my office and frantically, and without explanation, asked Jill to: "Call the Bishop of London!" Some moments later I could see the poor woman was looking totally perplexed. "Which one?" she enquired. "There's only one," I replied. "Richard Chartres." "Oh, the man, not the pub!" said Jill.

If it was hard for Jill, then it was equally tricky for David Lowe. The world of brokers — with their large egos and maverick approach — made it difficult for administrators such as David Lowe. Our employees at this stage were pretty indisciplined and disorganised, seeing admin as a "necessary evil". They completed their paperwork under a certain amount of pressure as it didn't come naturally to them

David, in fact, came to be known as the "Father Confessor" as a steady stream of brokers would beat a path to his office to admit they had done this, or failed to do that, in respect to some aspect of the running of the office, and sought absolution of their sins!

By every measure, we were becoming a substantial company and, inevitably, things like administration and strategy took on an added importance; board meetings gained a new impetus because we could see the way the markets were going. By 1983 I was working on the dealing board until 4pm and then spending two hours on administration. But as the new products came along, it soon became obvious that it was time for me to step back from the broking side — quite simply, I just couldn't afford the time.

Indeed, I was wanted elsewhere again. This time I spent three months working in Chicago to prepare us for the futures market here and when the London International Financial Futures Exchange (LIFFE) opened in London in 1982 — which was one of the decade's landmark events — we had a very big and successful futures team which brought about a lot of growth. As a result of the arrival of the futures market, an options market grew. The swaps market followed and by the late 80s these derivative products were being traded daily in many billions of dollars.

The ceremony of the signing of the Tokyo Forex deal was orchestrated and formal. We went to Hakone, a popular resort surrounding a lake on which large 18th century galleons take tourists on sightseeing trips. The actual signing was very colourful and included the traditional exchange of pens followed by a Samurai warrior using a sword to slice of the top of a

champagne cork. The ceremony was followed by a sumptuous
dinner and fine wines. I slept well that night, albeit that my
pillow was made of china and that my bed was rock solid!

The Japanese connection was to mean many trips to Tokyo
over the years. On one trip I recall a memorable occasion at
dinner with senior directors from the Bank of Tokyo during
which I found something green and unrecognisable on my plate.
So I asked the waiter what it was. And he didn't know.
Undaunted, I tried the Maitre D. And he didn't know. So, there
was nothing left for it but to turn to the chef. And, you've
guessed it, he didn't know either! We were to discover later that
it was some form of compressed seaweed. But that wasn't the
end of the fun. For dessert that night we were served strips of
jelly dipped in treacle. The trouble was we were expected to use
chopsticks! Needless to say, I had a success rate of about 10% —
with a lot more down my front than down my throat! When I
got back to the hotel I simply threw away my shirt and tie.

The Tokyo Forex merger meant big changes were afoot.
With David Riley gone, new management was coming through
to join people like Peter Doney and Colin Probets to steer us
through the 80s. The existing five directors were supplemented
with Alan Styant, Ken Yanagita and Yukio Kanno and this line-
up remained pretty well unchanged until 1987 when several
more directors were introduced: David Tuffley, Richard Magee,
Stephen Otterburn, Neil Humphreys and David Lowe. Over
the next two years — and at differing times as they came to
London — Hajime Moriyama, Tusugio Kambara, Kunio
Osugio and K. Koiumi also joined the board.

While this board arrangement might appear cumbersome, it
worked well. We were still, essentially, in our original premises,
which had been enlarged substantially by knocking through to
Ormond House next door. We had taken another complete
floor to cater for 500 staff and we were still growing. We moved

to Cable House in New Broad Street in 1990 and at that stage we were major brokers in spot and forward foreign exchange with approximately 200 brokers. But after 1993 when the Electronic Broking System (EBS) started, those numbers dwindled until today when Tullett has, by comparison, only a handful of people on spot foreign exchange. The forward market remains a hybrid-broked market — that is, voice and automated deal-matching — and, as a result of which, staff levels have declined by about 20%.

The late 70s had seen a burst of expansion. In 1978 we moved into Canada, the Middle East and Singapore followed by Hong Kong a year later. We then had a presence in Belgium and Sydney along with new relationships in Germany, Luxembourg and Paris. Further ahead, in the late 90s, we were to build up a relationship with companies in South America and South Africa.

The merged Tullett & Tokyo Forex had been looking east to China with a view to setting up an office. I had visited China in the 80s with Ken Yanagita to check out the prospects of establishing an operation in Beijing. We were guests of the Bank of China, which kindly provided their private guest rooms. Mine could have managed a party of at least 150 people! The hospitality was excellent, although I found the breakfast difficult to digest: sea slugs in warm water were, sadly, not for me. However, this was a minor detail compared with the friendships made from this visit.

By now, we were a multi-product global company, which had developed its strategy on the growing integration between markets. We repositioned our products to allow a closer physical presence between these related products and we were positioned to offer prices for these linked products.

Further, we could see that communications and information technology systems were essential to the development of a successful broking house. We planned to equip all offices with advanced communications tested in London and linked to the existing and highly-developed Tullett international network, so enabling dealers globally to receive prices in volatile international markets.

The opening of the representative office in Shanghai in 1997 — brought about by close collaboration with the People's Bank of China and other potential partners — helped to retain and develop contacts there and was an integral part of our international business strategy. We saw opening up in China as a way of monitoring its major cities and be in a position to make appropriate representations to areas where we thought we might assist in the development of the market.

Overall, the Shanghai representative office went well. We continued to use Hong Kong — with its marketing team — as our central base in Asia reinforced by senior personnel, including myself, who would try to get there twice a year. Another change at that time saw Benny Luk take over Far East responsibilities from Bruce Collins, when he returned to London. We had formed good relationships, including one with the China Foreign Exchange Trading System.

However, in the 80s another significant development was that academic standards right across the field of financial services were rising dramatically. Early on, we tended to employ people with market backgrounds, with personality and commitment

In the late 80s we required excellent A-levels and degrees. We never quite got round to saying to young recruits: "You have to have a degree" — but we were pretty close to it. This was a response to the fact that our clients had increased their academic requirements due to the arrival of highly-technical products like derivatives. By the end of the decade we were one of the top four brokers and considered to be part of the establishment — a long way from the early 70s when we were seen as new, brash, clever and innovative.

As we grew we could see a gap opening up between the

dealing room and the management. So we decided to bring back Les Brock, a seasoned broker, to form a new link between the two — a task that soon grew into a full-time personnel role and, with it, became the embryonic human resources section.

Les arrived to a situation in which morale among the brokers was pretty good with incomes and bonuses still attractive. But Les soon saw that an all-round recruitment policy was desperately needed with retention a key issue. At one level we were poaching broker talent from our rivals, which was fine. At another level, though, we were bringing in junior staff, but failing to retain them, which was a ridiculously expensive and disconcerting exercise and could not be allowed to continue.

At one stage, with an establishment of around 1,000 staff, we were turning over some 500 people a year, a large percentage of which were from our back office staff. Even so, there was something of a "revolving door" culture, with brokers coming and going at a spectacular rate. For example, we were leaking graduates.

We were a training company and as our trainees became experienced and began to fulfil their potential as quality brokers and possible management, our competitors were poaching them. Les Brock, I know, felt this was down to apathy among some senior staff towards a graduate intake. The view of management was that senior staff should employ quality to make themselves "redundant". Not that we could, because this was a stepping stone to serious management.

But by becoming the size we were towards the end of the 80s, we also stopped being the good innovators of the early part of the decade when the new products came on line. We were still number one in a number of products, but had fallen behind in many others and catching up proved hard to do.

Size also meant we were becoming a difficult company to manage. So we decided to restructure the management into a two-tier system: on one level we had heads of divisions responsible for day-to-day operations with the international board responsible for strategy and a number of items identified and reserved to the board.

But the management, in my view, took on the feel of old-style personality brokers because, quite simply, they weren't prepared to find out about and understand the products. There was one director who treated the staff under him as his friends and would do anything to keep them. What he should have been saying was: "These people are not performing, we have to change." Unfortunately, there were several like him on the board and their influence stayed around for a number of years and held back our development.

I have never believed in contracts, albeit all our employees were contracted to the company. If an employee does not wish to work with the company we should not attempt to hang on to him. A naïve view, perhaps, but one based on my own loyalty to those with whom I have been employed during my career.

As a result, there was a continual battle to upgrade the management. The four involved should have gone in the early or middle 80s — but the board could not afford to lose four in one go. When the company first started, decision-making was relatively easy among a few like-minded directors, such as David, Peter and myself. But as the company grew, and with it the board, decision-making became more difficult. We went through a difficult period of about five years in the mid-80s — a time when I was travelling throughout the year.

It was during this time that one of the trickiest episodes in my business career occurred, which again reflected the poor period that the company was going through. What came to be known as the "Brussels affair" could have ruined the company, as any whiff of scandal would have wrecked our credibility.

For some time we had operated an office in Belgium which,

apart from being a potentially useful profit centre in itself, showed how important we viewed Brussels as a significant financial centre and important in any future European Union. In short, we felt that there were very good reasons for being there.

Initially, we had been approached by a couple of brokers whom we had done business with. We knew them to be good brokers from a good company. What we didn't realise was the extent of the corruption in the Belgium market. All European markets have problems and it would be naive to say that London hasn't had its share.

In a secondary manner, I guess we joined in the game in Belgium because we employed people who acted on our behalf in companies in a correspondent relationship. The two brokers concerned had turned themselves into companies, which is not an unusual thing to do in Belgium. In effect, they were self-employed and became consultants for us — so we paid their company.

At this time, we didn't understand the way deals worked in Belgium. A broker organising, say, the borrowing of $10m for a year would receive commission from the dealers. The broker would then pay 25-30% of it back to the dealer. So we employed these two brokers and they employed other people, and operated in this way. Not surprisingly, it was a very successful company.

I must say I had suspicions about the whole system there, but had no proof of wrong-doing. Having suspicions is one thing; being able to make accusations stick is another.

What was happening in Brussels came to light as a direct result of our changing accountants. The new team at KMPG started to examine basic things in the accounts in the Brussels office and found a couple of innocent-looking items that were eventually to set the alarm bells ringing. They spotted the fact that we had direct lines into certain banks in Europe for which we paid the rentals, but from which we appeared to be getting no income. "Why was this?" Answer: "We, don't know." The reason, it turned out, was that those payments were staying offshore and finally coming back in the form of cash.

All this came out into the open after we dismissed a fairly senior member of our Brussels set-up. In an attempt to gain revenge, he then went to the authorities and told them we were paying "commissions" on deals and concealing them. In Belgium, bribery was legal as long as you paid the tax.

Before this blew up I had been visiting the Brussels office once a month just to look at the figures, but even this I think it's fair to say put me on the fringes of the operation there. In advance of my regular trip to Belgium, we were informed that I would need to attend a meeting there with the tax authorities. I took it on face value, not realising the seriousness of what lay ahead. Perhaps I should have? Perhaps I should have read the situation better and stayed in London, so preventing the crisis that developed. Anyway, I didn't and set off for Brussels.

So, in November 1986 I embarked on a routine monthly trip to Belgium only to be greeted when I arrived at the office with a phone call from the police, asking me to come down to the their headquarters to answer some questions.

The directors thought that "Brussels" would be very serious for the company. For when you are dealing with banks and, as brokers, on the basis of trust, any suggestion that you are paying commission to banks' dealers to conduct business could be calamitous. How would banks around the world know that the problem was confined solely to Belgium? And if you lose your credit lines with clearing banks, you have no business.

In Belgian law, the head of a company is the company and so the authorities, quite naturally, wanted to speak to me. For my part, I was an unlimited partner of Tullett & Tokyo Belgium and, although I was entirely liable for the company, I was, in turn, indemnified by the company for all eventualities.

I agreed to the police request, thinking that assisting them with their enquiries was no big deal. At the beginning of the interview they told me they had our managing director in another room and that my answers to their questions needed to match his.

"Did I know that the company was doing deals outside Belgium and that the money was being collected offshore?" (which isn't necessarily illegal). "Did I know that these contracts had either been destroyed or been stored in a secret place?" To which I replied: "No, I didn't know this. Why should I? I couldn't possibly have known this. This is absolute news to me. I only get the figures from our accountants on a monthly basis and which we analyse."

Although, as I say, I did have a feeling something might have been going on, I had no proof. Until I knew the number or the name of the accounts involved I would not have been able to prove it. As it turned out, the account involved was named Tullet 2, which further suggested to the police that I was involved and that I was receiving the money. All I can say is that if I had been involved I wouldn't have called the account Tullett 2!

The police said that this money was being used to pay for commission, both in Belgium and outside. "Do you realise the tax implications?" they asked. "Yes, I did."

At that point, the police had some discussions among themselves and, on returning, said: "Do you realise that your managing director doesn't say the same as you? I replied: " I don't have anything to say, I have told you what I know." They stepped up the pressure. "The managing director said that you knew what was going on." I repeated that I did not know what was going on and that this was all a surprise to me.

"We are going to have to put you in prison tonight." So, I said: "OK, but I'd better ring my wife and tell her what's happening and I need to speak to my lawyers." "No, you can only make one telephone call." So, I called Anita and told her I was being kept in prison overnight and she seemed as relaxed as me about the whole thing. I asked her to contact a lawyer friend who lived near Brussels and explained the situation to him. I also told her to call the company and tell them what had happened.

Immediately the company heard I was being held, it wanted to issue a press release as part of a damage limitation exercise. Luckily, we had an excellent lawyer in Bernard Bartlett of Berwin Leighton. Bernard asked the directors three key questions: Does the situation stop you trading? Does it affect your creditworthiness with suppliers and customers? Do you owe a duty of care to clients to make such a statement? And, of course, the answer was no to each of them. So he persuaded us that public comment would be the wrong thing and that we should say nothing, go about our business in the usual way and review the situation daily.

Apparently, prison was only going to be overnight. It was to be some 20 days later before they let me out. Early on I spoke to my Belgian lawyer and said: "You've got to get me out of here." He thought that I would probably be detained for between 10 and 20 days, so he was correct there. I was kept in a prison, rather than in cells at the police station. It was at the better end of that prison fortunately, among those who were considered to be of no risk to the community. Just to add to the fun the prison authorities deprived me of water for some reason which led to my having kidney problems.

While all this was going on there was natural concern within the company about my plight and Anita was particularly anxious having brought our sons to see me — and, as you can imagine, that was certainly upsetting for me seeing them in that situation.

Even though I knew I was innocent, it was certainly a worrying time and very much a low point in my career. After 20 days I was released. The police, having questioned the two Belgian executives concerned, found the contracts and the offshore company they were looking for. As it was a tax offence, the company was fined and that was the end of the matter for the time being.

With hindsight, I think the police had been waiting to pounce and it would have been on the next Tullett executive arriving in Belgium. It just happened to be me. But even if it had not have been, they would certainly have had to have prosecuted me personally, as I was the company representative.

It was only towards the end of my near-three week incarceration that the media got to hear about it. For most of that time, it seems, nobody in the industry queried where I was and, if they noted my absence, the company simply said I was on holiday. But suddenly the news about my arrest was leaked to Belgian television and one small bank closed our line of credit until the situation was clarified. The majority of banks, however, stood by us. They didn't believe the corruption claims because of my standing as chairman and my reputation in the industry. I discovered that, when it heard about my plight, the Bank of England also sought to intervene on my behalf.

So, I was released much to everybody's relief and the business fall-out was actually minimal. But there was a radical fall-out within the company in both Brussels and London. As a result of this episode, we replaced the MD in Brussels, who theoretically set up the whole corrupt arrangement, and brought in Patrick Annez, whom I had known for years. I knew he was very reliable and trustworthy, but still felt the need to ask him rhetorically: "This will never happen again, will it Patrick?"

Corruption was not an issue in London: we had to justify all expense for clients, which amounted to various forms of entertainment. Corporate entertaining at sports events or taking clients for a meal were OK, but things like nightclubs were not.

Either way, we were expected to entertain sensibly and not go over the top. In those days, the Bank of England regulated the City with a "wink and a nod" approach and if it thought there was a little too much entertaining going on, it would make its views known — without having to put it in writing — and we cut back as a result. The Bank was a very powerful organisation and when it spoke, you listened. We were all very circumspect about the Bank; its form of regulation worked very well, until the FSA took over regulatory duties from it.

Corruption in Belgium, on the other hand, was an issue: it was part of the business culture. Part of the problem was that the taxes were so high there, which encouraged people to take advantage of any opportunity of cash. In the futures market, whenever an order came in from Belgium, we used to say: "It's the Belgian dentist, again!" A reference to the fact that he was the only one who ever had any money, because he never declared his clients to the authorities.

During Patrick's stewardship in Brussels, things began to change. The market had moved on and we had become a limited liability company and I'd like to think that the "commission" problem stopped. His time as managing director didn't last long as he was tragically killed in a motorcycle accident.

After that we decided to close our Belgium operations. Although the business culture had changed for the better, profits from Brussels had fallen to 5% of revenues, which hardly made it worthwhile continuing. So we sold the business to the management there and dealt with our trading in Belgium from our London office.

The Belgium episode reflected the different way of trading that existed in Europe then. Dealers expected a payback from their local brokers, but not from their UK or American brokers. Northern Europe, particularly Scandinavia, doesn't get involved in this behaviour as they used to do in Italy, France, Spain and

Portugal, where the attitude is: "What's in it for me?" The Bank of England was very well aware of this and we made it clear what was happening. I believe this has improved and I like to think that it does not happen today.

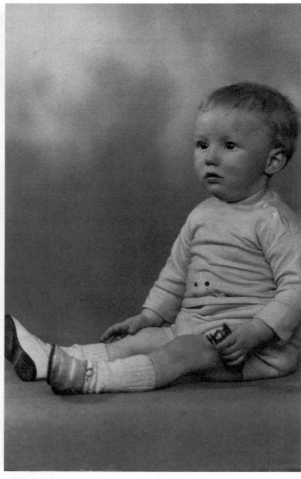

My parents, Percy and Vera,
on their wedding day

Baby days

With my mother Vera
in May 1943

On Service in Malaya

My 21st birthday party

Kohima Platoon (front row third from left) after six weeks training at Stoughton Barracks, Guildford in 1953

First meeting of FEBA around 1955, from the left: Reg Winterbourne, Wally Godsell, Reg Saville, Brian Cole, Ted Lloyd, George Galloway, Freddie Souch, Vivian Pearce, "Jacko" Jackson, Bill Heath and Gerald Baer

Medieval banquet to mark my 50th birthday

Tullett & Riley: the early years

Golfing day with colleagues Jim Moriyama, Ken Yanagita and Soh Kim Huat

My mother and father, late 1980s

Day at the Palace: Investiture by Prince Charles

Kevin and Jonathan take in the atmosphere

My precious CBE

Whitgift School 1st XV 1951-52 (back row, second from left)

My Uncle Dick and Aunt Patricia on their wedding day, early 1950s

Glenn and Karen

Neil and Lynn

At my combined "70th birthday and 50 years in the City"
party celebrating with Gloria and Lord and Lady Levy

Co-driving with Alan Gaunt in the Trans-Sahara Rally 1974

Polka Theatre time with teenagers
Jonathan and Kevin

With Gloria on my graduation day, City University

Graduation day with Neil, Glenn and Jonathan

Reception for City Guild with Lord Mayor David Brewer and William and Valerie Brake 2006

Ski-ing in Annapurna

Tree planting with Baroness Rothschild in 1996

Doubles match with squash partner Ray Rook (far left) and opponents Brian Sayer and Keith Spurgeon

Formula 3 racing in early 1970s

6

THE MATURITY

Despite the Brussels affair, the company could look back over the 1980s with some satisfaction on a job well done. We had emerged from our infancy and youth with a few growing pains but had made it to maturity. Tullett & Tokyo International had embraced great changes in products along the way. Looking back, a lot of the problems we ran into in the 80s were purely the unavoidable growing pains of a young and successful company and to that extent were unavoidable.

Overall, by the end of the 80s — and despite the problems along the way — I happily settled for the position that the company found itself in. If anything, we were a shade better than we anticipated — although we remained in awe of the three major companies in the field, feeling that they still represented the model of where we should be and what we should be doing.

The 90s began with a stream of changes. We were moving from our original home to new offices in Cable House, New Broad Street, but we were also about to undergo a major shake-up in the boardroom.

Brussels had led to much soul-searching within the company. How could this incident possibly have happened? As chairman of Brussels, I had operational responsibility, which arose from a role that had probably been madness for me to take on in the first place: quite simply, it was not possible to commit enough time to it. But even if I had had the time, I doubt if I could have spotted what was going on. Anyway, when things went pear-shaped I was seriously exposed and that couldn't be allowed to happen again.

It was a seminal moment for the company and a lot of the boardroom instability stemmed from it. For now, changes were demanded and Alan Styant, for one, wanted to see someone brought in from outside to become chairman. He felt it was too much for me to be chairman and chief executive and called for an independent chairman to be appointed; however, we again appointed from within.

In the 70s when the business was first formed, decision-making was done sort of "on the hoof" but with all the directors involved. Up to this point I think I can honestly say that I knew everybody in the dealing room and they knew me. But, when I became chairman and chief executive, my style of management became, inevitably, more remote. After all, I was travelling the world visiting our operations making contact and forging new relationships with brokers.

Belgium's problems had arisen even though I was regularly visiting the Brussels office. Travel was taking up too much time, so I deliberately cut back because we had board difficulties at home and London was the key to everything: we needed a strong London to be strong internationally.

The boardroom team that began the decade remained in place until 1992, when Peter Bertram joined as a non-executive director to be followed later by John Lawrence. Company accountant Philip Gregory became finance director in 1995 and, within two years, we appointed Tim Boyle from New York and Seichi Akiyama from Tokyo.

Increasingly, we were to have a board that was split and, in that situation, vacuums can arise and black holes created where information goes missing. In the late 80s and late 90s we went through episodes where information was deliberately withheld by certain directors — and, of course, management power resides with those directors who are in the know. These directors were getting information and not sharing it with other members of the board.

At this time we couldn't afford for the directors involved — who were all resisting certain things — to all resign at the same time and so the rest of the board and I had to give in to their style of management, while trying to be positive. They were a group of negative thinkers who were earning good salaries without having to work particularly hard. They were good ambassadors to our clients because they were personalities, but they were terrible ambassadors in-house where they behaved with arrogance.

To some extent the boardroom strife was linked to the struggle we were having with product innovation — for example, one director said futures and derivatives were not our traditional business. But, of course, they were the key to the future. This was an example of a complete lack of understanding of the products. These people were not prepared to sit down and develop product knowledge; therefore, when they spoke to clients about these products they could not do so authoritatively. I sensed that the boardroom difficulties were becoming apparent to the staff, although nothing was ever said to me.

Board meetings had always been exciting and a place where difficult decisions often had to be taken, but where one could debate without acrimony. However, during that era things became very unpleasant. With hindsight we should have just said "go" and taken the heavy knock and coped with the difficulty that the loss of four directors would have given to our credibility. I'm pretty certain we would have overcome that very quickly.

One of the mistakes that we made was that by increasing the membership of the board we took on people who were good at their job without knowing whether they could be good at management. We were hopelessly wrong and should have looked for good management material instead. It was typical of the times that good brokers were kept on by their companies and turned into directors.

We were one of the first to drop this idea and we told people who threatened to leave unless they were made directors, that they could go because we would not be making them directors. Another procedure we had adopted, which was not the correct thing to do, saw three of us meet on a regular basis to discuss wider issues: this was another sign of the split on the board.

Finally, the resignation and retirement of those that had diversified the board for many years, resulted in a new line-up of totally-committed and loyal directors and I wondered if this would prove to be the end of our board problems.

Fortunately, the 1990s saw us leave behind the relative market stagnation of the late 80s and what, for us, was a poor period in our history. We got back and started to grow and were innovative again: we created an executive committee! The board managed the company and created the strategy and gave management parameters to the committee who, in turn, managed that strategy. It was a good structure and worked well for us and it's an arrangement that still exists today. We called it a committee as it was not another board of directors. The management improved once we had put this structure in place.

We had been well prepared for the "Big Bang" in the City in 1986-87 and our equities side had made a great success of it. As far as gilts were concerned, what we didn't realise was that the market was personality-based. We had started in gilts with quality employees. We then had to go into the street and "buy" two personality brokers. To some extent we were putting the clock back, but that's typical of the money market, which goes in cycles. It seems to operate in about five-year cycles of personality and non-personality broking. By the time we had employed our two "personality" brokers, the tide was turning and the market required the skilled broker.

Negotiable commissions had arrived in the 80s, and along with several other companies, we argued that we should be able to charge what we liked. The FEBA said we would be undercutting and commissions would drop in all companies and that we would all be charging the same commission but lower than previously. Our response was that, as long as we are happy with our profits, that would be OK. We were also told at one time to limit our entertaining. "Does that mean you want us to do all our entertaining down at Starbucks?" we thought. And as a further sign of the interfering culture within the FEBA at the time, it also stopped a company working for a week because they had poached talented brokers from rivals!

Business is done in all sorts of ways and lavish entertainment can still go on — for example, these days some companies transact business with clients on nights out at lap dancing clubs! We can't dictate what people want to do, but we're not prepared to pay for it. Today's market is in every way — technology, quality of the people and the knowledge they have — a much better market than it was 20 years ago. Brokers are able to give intelligent answers to client questions and gone are the days when, in reply to an enquiry about why the market had gone down, a client would be told: "More sellers than buyers, mate!"

Though we were putting some of the difficulties of the previous years behind us, an enormous test was just around the corner. In what was to be the watershed moment for the markets, September 1993 would see the introduction of the

Electronic Broking System (EBS). The system had been about 15 months in development and was launched by a consortium of 14 banks which included Barclays, Midland and NatWest from Britain and Citibank, JP Morgan and Lehman Bros from America and the Union Bank of Switzerland (UBS).

When the system was launched, some people thought that automatic deal-matching was a temporary phenomenon and would not last. As one senior broker famously said at the time: "It won't buy you lunch, will it!" It may not have been able to buy lunch but it changed the workings of the market forever.

But it's fair to say that when EBS was introduced few could see that it would necessarily break the mould in the way we conducted business. None of the companies in the spot foreign exchange market knew exactly what would happen; none of us knew how initially to react to it. The earliest figures that we got from Singapore showed that approximately 3% of spot foreign exchange business went through the brokers there, who previously enjoyed a total monopoly of the market.

I deal with EBS in more detail in the chapter that follows. But sufficient to say here, it revolutionised trading and, almost overnight, dealt a severe blow to the traditional spot foreign exchange market.

That said, from the earliest days of electronic deal-matching I was confident that, even if it was here to stay, there would always be a smaller role for old-style "voice" transactions — though not so much in foreign exchange. You know what you get with foreign exchange: it's bland, straightforward and has two prices a bid and an offer! And today most spot trading is a "hybrid" mix of voice and electronic deal-matching.

EBS made a real mark but, fortunately, did not sweep all before it, as it might have done. A number of things may have checked its progress. Another early question mark raised against EBS came in the shape of name risk. But, experience would show that there was virtually none. So long as it's a recognised name, you rarely get a name turned down on spot.

On forwards, it's slightly different. You may be looking six months forward, so you're taking a risk on that name for six months. All banks have limits to the amount they can deal in — particularly deposits. The large banks have sizeable limits for each other on spot foreign exchange, which enables the markets to deal in large amounts. If the management of EBS had, at this time, elected to diversify into other products, today's broking market would be a different place and worth more than ICAP recently paid.

I think people overreact to derivatives. Such products never really worried me, but I understand there are limits to the business that can be done.

In the mid-90s we built an arbitrage area to look at the whole of the picture and very often they would see an arbitrage situation arise that could transact a deal — however, it would mean doing three or four deals to consummate the trade. The client may reject three deals and want to take it with two and, hopefully, the deal could be transacted with marginal improvements in price from all concerned.

The arbitrage area was very important for us and, in fact, our New York software team designed a system called "The Beast" which was ahead of its time, but never a big earner and which we eventually sold as we didn't have the funds to continue developing it. The Beast had a page called the Prairie, which was a three-dimensional object on the screen and was continually moving and changing shape. It was brownish on the bottom and red on one of the peaks and then it would go to amber and then to green on which the broker would click on to. It would then tell you exactly how one traded at a market price using several products. If you chose the amber it would tell you to watch out for certain aspects; green offered the optimum moment. In those days, it was one of the most innovative pieces of software that I'd seen. It was amazing for its time!

In bringing new products to the market there is always fierce rivalry between companies and research is done in the strictest secrecy. I can recall just one occasion in the money markets when information was pooled between the broking companies. This came about in the late 1960s after the chairman of FEBA failed to pass on information he had that we would be able to deal in Eurodollars outside of the UK. He had all his team out there in Europe before he decided to tell the other association members about it.

Understandably, the association reacted angrily. As a result, it set up a joint company called FEBA Ltd, which was to last for a year. FEBA was made up of people from different companies and I represented Savage & Heath. The company pooled all the deals from the brokers. The man in charge of it was Wing Commander Ted Jackman, DFC, who, rather unwisely I felt, insisted on having all his RAF details on his business card — this, at a time, when we were trying to get into Germany, Italy and Austria!

After EBS there had to be changes. In the money markets, if brokers are making money they are, generally speaking, happy. But after EBS it was harder to earn money on the spot market as it had become far more competitive. The company had to be more structured as our finances were looked at more closely and, in common, with our rivals, we appointed a finance director, rather than an accountant. We were in a new era and as one senior broker observed: "We're all accountants now!"

On the management side of things, there was still some strife in the boardroom and eventually this led to Mike Everett's resignation. Alan Styant firmly believed at this stage that we needed to bring in someone who, if not outside the company, should at least be from outside London. The business had become increasingly complex with a series of areas to cater for — such as, forex, futures etc. In addition, Tulletts had regionalised with Europe, Asia and North American centres. Alan Styant was in charge of Asia, Richard Magee ran North America and David Tuffley ran Europe. And it was to Richard, or Rick as he was known, that the company turned and he came in as chairman in 1991.

Rick, who had run our New York office, had been a real success story having joined at the outset as a trainee broker. Rick joined the Tullett group in August 1971 after having been in the Merchant Navy for 12 to 13 years, becoming qualified as a Master Mariner on foreign-going vessels in June 1968. He had played football with Peter Doney, who approached me about his joining us. Rick recalls that he only had to observe Peter's lifestyle and attitude to conclude that money broking would suit him.

His talent and enthusiasm for all things American saw him progress quickly to the US and he became MD of our New York operation in 1980 and in 1991 he transferred to Tokyo to create the first foreign broker in government securities.

Rick was a skilled operator, but I recall one moment when he was almost wrong-footed. It came at dinner during a six-monthly Tullett conference, on this occasion in Singapore. He ordered frogs legs and asked if they were fresh. And I can see his face now as his enquiry was answered in the background by the sound of crunching legs and squealing frogs!

His appointment was announced at the company's 21st anniversary dinner in London, where he told the audience in typically witty and modest fashion: "It's strange to think I was once a little trainee — and now I'm a little chairman!" With his appointment, I continued as President stepping back from the day-to-day hurly burly and adopting a more strategic role.

Rick did a good job for us at a difficult time: he worked hard and managed to carry the board with him. He also persuaded Alan Styant to give up the Asia job, which he loved, and return to London. In joining the main board, Alan looked after securities, which had run into a certain amount of difficulty.

By 1996, Tullett & Tokyo Forex had made pre-tax profits of £11.5m, which doubled the following year to £22.1m. At this time I was president of the company and, at the age of 62, I was moving away from the frontline of the business and beginning, what was to be, the "long goodbye".

After being chairman for four years, Rick decided to retire in 1996. With Rick's departure, Alan Styant was sounded out about the chairmanship but, at 52, decided it was not for him. Instead, we appointed John Nixon who came to us from Toronto with a good reputation, but our stalwart core of four or five directors, who were proving difficult in other respects, didn't really get on with him.

John had many attributes and had a lot going for him. As well as being a talented businessman, he was very sociable and all-round sportsman — particularly skiing, squash and tennis. In the two years he was with us, John was very hot on forward thinking in terms of company strategy. But his appointment split the board yet again. Some saw him as rather autocratic and felt he had failed to hold the confidence of his regional directors, in particular.

There followed mumblings about John's management style and eventually, the resignation of a senior member of staff in New York brought the whole issue out into the open and John left. Despite differences in the office, John was liked socially and many felt he handled himself in a very professional manner when he stood down. These days he is an advisor to the company's biggest rival, ICAP.

Somewhat later, the board's "stalwarts" all retired at the same time, which enabled us to regroup as a management and allowed the company to move on. By 1999 the board boasted four more additions, fully reflecting the growing influence of our Japanese partners: Kimotoshi Yasui, Hiroyuki Kuroda, Koichi Yamamoto and, crucially as it turned out, Bruce Collins.

By the mid-90s, when the markets had changed so dramatically, people like David Lowe and Peter Doney, decided it was time to leave and their departure pretty well brought to an end the era of those senior staff who had been with the company since its formative days.

When he retired, David Lowe had been Finance Director for four years and seen the company through one of its biggest crises in that period when the banks, faced with mounting bad debts, tightened up on lending conditions and we lost our arrangements with Barclays. David had sole responsibility for dealing with this and it took him six months of painstaking work to put together a new £25m credit line with another bank — vital to the company at a time of heavy investment in communications and IT. This was probably David's finest hour.

Although EBS had led to tougher market conditions in the 1990s, there was still a good working atmosphere in the company and morale on the dealing floor was good. It was harder to make money, but the company was still reasonably successful at it.

As the decade came to an end we were still making tidy profits in what was proving a much tougher market post-EBS. In 1998 Tullett & Toyko Forex posted pre-tax profits of £19.5m, which dropped 12 months later to £6.3m, when special factors were at play.

Even though winding down to retirement, I was still active in the company. I was putting together the whole of the Tullett corporate governance and it was a fairly time consuming period as I chaired the board which met to determine strategy. I always gave myself a week to prepare for a board meeting, which was a lesson I learned early on and still stick to. Despite the boardroom difficulties, we had managed to progress. In fact, in our Executive Committee we had a lot of talent and the strategy that was given to them was a good basic one. It behaved like good management and everybody knew what was happening. In wider terms, we had come to accept through the 80s and 90s that a bumpy ride would be part of our journey. Indeed, the next bumpy bit was not far away and there was a profound sense of deja vu about it.

We had taken over the Liberty Brokerage operation in New York and I was out there when a full-blown crisis blew up in 1999. In a re-run of the situation we faced in the early 80s, vital project information was withheld from the board.

The problem surrounded the development of electronic deal-matching systems for securities. The introduction of EBS in London seven years earlier had certainly caught us out and so we were keen to have something of our own. But Cantor was developing eSpeed and ICAP was working on a system of its own. This put these two well ahead of the rest and the best we could hope for our system would to be third in the field.

Even so, we faced three big problems. The core of the system was not of a high enough quality to do the job; Cantor and Reuters warned us we would be hit with patent claims; and, worst of all, the project was soaking up money. We learned, eventually, that it was going to cost us approaching $50m to put together, without it being marketed and everything else that goes with launching a new product. In addition to that heavy cost, you've then got a two- year lag before you are ready to go to market and in that time people are saying what does yours do that the others don't? And, of course, the answer was — nothing.

So, I looked at this and talked to Bruce Collins and said this isn't going to work is it? He agreed and I then spoke to Ken Yanagita who was a major shareholder and explained to him what was happening. Ken told me he'd lost all faith in the current management. I said to him: "Ken, do you realise what you've just said? You, as a major shareholder, are saying to the current senior operations management: 'You have to resign'." I told him he would have to repeat what he'd said to the next board meeting.

He did just that and the Chief Executive resigned. Our Finance Director stayed on for nine months to give us time to find a replacement and there was a two-month overlap when we eventually brought in Stephen Jack.

This episode showed that not enough homework had been done and decisions were made without proper costing — and this information was kept from other members of the board. After some investigations, which I began, we discovered that software and marketing was eating up money at a rate we could not sustain. We decided we really couldn't afford this and so had to pull the plug on the project.

The crisis over the deal-matching project saw my recall to the frontline of the business — a situation I had not expected. So, I returned as Chairman and Bruce Collins, who had been managing director of our Far East operations, came in as Chief Executive. It was up to Bruce and myself to set about repairing the damage and, having spent $25m to date, the first thing we did was to see if we could salvage bits of the system for our use. So, it was a major decision to just abandon the whole thing. Not surprisingly, in 2000 the company reported pre-tax losses of £10.8m.

It had been one of the biggest crises the company had faced and the next thing we had to do was reassure our investors. We had four American shareholders, who came to us through Liberty, and between them they owned 20% of the company. I immediately appointed one executive from each of the American investors to the board as non-executive directors. I told them that we were going to need help and they made a great success of things through direct business and investment guarantees to the point where we were able to turn things around and in 2001 we made profits of £27.7m.

Through our US merger we grew into Tullett & Tokyo Liberty and grew steadily over the next few years. At this time we were employing around 2,000 people in the main financial centres in Europe, North and South America, Asia and Australia. By now, we were also a leading player in fixed-income securities and had become involved in the energy and oil broking fields. In 2001 we made a profit of £27m and in 2002 upped that to £35m. We had become the second largest inter-dealer broker, after ICAP, by overtaking Cantor Fitzgerald, the US government bond broker, which suffered badly in the 9/11 attacks on the World Trade Centre.

Since its inception, Tulletts had been evolving slowly and organically and its culture with it. The merger with Liberty, however, had brought about more dramatic changes, particularly in the way we were perceived outside the company. For instance, though we had remained a private company from the outset, there were constant press reports that we were about to be taken over by a number of our rivals.

We saw ourselves in vigorous shape and looking to an independent future. I had long preferred a stock market flotation — indeed only the Brussels affair previously prevented this — which would have valued the company at more than £200m. As we appointed a firm to advise on an initial public offering (IPO), Bruce commented to our colleagues and shareholders: "We continue to consider a number of options and opportunities to enable us to sustain Tullett's growth and progress, including an IPO."

With Stephen Jack's arrival as Chief Finance Officer in October 2001, we had someone with a fine City pedigree. He was appointed to the board with a view to helping organise a possible stock market listing. A sub committee comprising Bruce Collins, Stephen Jack, David Clark as an independent non-executive director, and myself, was set up to explore the possibilities.

One of the outcomes of the 9/11 tragedy was to underline how important the capital markets business was for the group and we were well positioned to benefit from the way in which the market changed. It soon became clear that the profitability of the company would offer us corporate opportunities that we needed to take seriously on behalf of our shareholders.

The sub committee appointed Amethyst as advisors, and we examined three main strategies: a merger with a major competitor; an IPO; a sale of the company. During the ensuing months we worked on the first two of these options both individually as projects but also with a view to an IPO after a merger. It was in the spring of 2002 that we were approached by Collins Stewart and the sub committee had to weigh up the relative benefits of quite different deals for both the short and the long term.

The press thought the impetus towards listing was understood to have come from the stock market success of Michael Spencer's ICAP since its reverse takeover of Garban in 1999. This was credited with opening the City's eyes to the attractions of inter-dealer brokers, whose earnings tend to be less volatile than conventional brokers.

But we became vulnerable to a takeover and inevitably we had our suitors. So much so that by September 2002 we had to formally acknowledge that we had received a takeover approach from stockbroker Collins Stewart and within a few months we had been merged, even though the company had not been for sale.

The shareholders, however, wanted to see liquidity in their

holdings and an exit route for their investments. The management of the business had been reformed and profitability had significantly improved and the shareholders would benefit anyway. But the sub committee analysis demonstrated clearly that a purchase merger by Collins Stewart would offer the best price for their holding. It was on this basis that, in January 2003, I recommended to the board the sale/merger of the company. I had spoken previously to the shareholders and assured myself that they were fully informed.

The major shareholders — which included Totan (Tokyo Forex's new name), the Japanese financial firm; Hermes, the former Post Office pension fund, which owned 10.5%; and American shareholders who held 20% — voted to accept the merger. A leading voice in those wanting to accept the Collins Stewart bid was New Media Spark, a venture capital firm led by Michael Whitaker, which held an 11% stake.

Bruce and I, on the other hand, believed there was still mileage in the company, as it existed. Despite difficult markets our half-year turnover had increased by 11% to £213m producing profits of just under £20m. Despite this, the board voted for the Collins Stewart deal which saw them pay £250m cash and equity for Tullett Liberty and so, some 32 years after I formed the company, it finally passed out of my hands.

After the 2003 deal I stayed on for a year or so with the new Collins Stewart Tullett as president of Tullett Liberty, later to become Tullett Prebon. By now, the group had used the foundations we had built to become a fully diversified inter-dealer broker with leading positions in fixed income securities, equities, energy, credit derivatives, global money, futures and capital markets with a global reach continuing to operate in 18 centres: London, New York, Hong Kong, Singapore, Tokyo, Frankfurt, Paris, Luxembourg, Sydney, Toronto, Warsaw, Zurich, Bahrain, Bangalore, Jakarta, Kuala Lumpur, Manila and Mumbai.

Soon after the deal with Collins Stewart, the company bought Prebon, adding another important brand name to its inter-dealing brokerage. Prebon was formed in 1990 following the merger of three leading London-based money brokers — Babcock & Brown, Kirkland-Whittaker and Fulton Prebon. Both the Tullett Liberty and Prebon brands operate on a "hybrid" system of electronic and voice broking services being provided to clients through direct lines to trading desks, supported by proprietary screen which display historical data, analysis and real time prices. As a postscript, in March 2006 it was announced that the Collins Stewart stockbroking business would be split from the Tullett Prebon money broking operation and floated separately on the stock market.

Anyway, I formally ended my full-time association with the company at the end of 2004, although I worked for them in a consultancy capacity for a short while after. Bruce, meanwhile, left Collins Stewart Tullett in April 2004, being replaced by Lou Scotto, who had been at the helm of Tullett in the US.

So, that was that. The company I founded in 1971 had gone on to achieve great things — from a standing start it had grown into the second largest money broker in the world, which was some achievement. I had had a wonderful time. There had been much excitement, some despair, good days, bad days, many friends made and miles travelled. We hadn't always gone down the right path, but we got far more right than we got wrong. And, at the end of it all, it remains the case that "the name's on the door" — a lasting achievement in itself.

Some 33 years after its launch, I left the good ship Tullett. It had been a great voyage, but as I came ashore, I took a deep breath and, with my newly found land legs, looked for adventures new.

7

THE WATERSHED

The meeting had gone well. Tullett's most senior personnel worldwide, faced with some key decisions, had gathered for a summit at a hotel and conference complex in southern Spain, far from the cool of a British autumn and the cares and pressures of the London marketplace. There had been many items on the agenda, but there was one that was taking up a lot of our thoughts: what to do about the new electronic deal-matching system which was threatening the company's core business. EBS — the Electronic Broking System — had been introduced by a consortium of banks and had revolutionised trading in what was clearly a defining moment for the broking industry.

There had been much tough talking over the three days. Worried about the effects of EBS, the meeting strove to agree a strategy to cope with the ground-breaking innovation which had begun to wreck the way the spot foreign exchange market was traditionally run. Automated trading was pulling a huge amount of business away from the traditional "voice" method and, in so doing, was threatening to destroy our foreign exchange revenues which were so important to us. We had to think the unthinkable and many jobs would probably have to go.

As they congratulated themselves on their deliberations over the three days, the directors contemplated a little well-earned leisure therapy on the Costa del Sol: a balmy evening full of good food, fine wine and a gentle letting down of the hair. The meeting was about to break up, their work done. Suddenly, international board member Ken Yanagita got to his feet and delivered his bombshell. He announced very coolly to his colleagues that the group's Japanese arm, Tokyo Forex, had been developing its own Minex spot deal-matching system and would be launching it in competition to EBS.

The assembled Tullett ranks had had no idea this was in the pipeline and were visibly shocked at the announcement. "You might have chosen a better moment," I told Ken. "You could have told us earlier. We should have discovered this before." Apparently, if we couldn't beat EBS, we were about to join them in a system that would change broking forever. The trip into town was cancelled and we talked on well into the night.

Although Tullett's directors met each year in this way, the Spanish conference of 1993 was, undoubtedly, a direct reaction to the launch of EBS, which had hit the market much like a missile landing on a defenceless target. We knew the 12 banks had been discussing such a move and had, indeed, joked with us, from time to time, saying: "Oh, we won't need you soon!" Some took such talk seriously, some didn't — like the short-sighted senior broker who proclaimed: "Well, it won't buy you lunch!" This was a reference to the fact that computers could do many things, but they couldn't connect with the dealers, in the way that traditional broking over the telephone offered that personal touch.

Other brokers, sceptical about such a far-reaching development, didn't think banks would be able to co-operate in an area in which they were such fierce rivals. Either way, we couldn't be sure what the banks were up to, but the period leading to the launch of EBS was intriguing and full of speculation. If the new system was so radical, it would wipe out much of what we had known. This was unthinkable wasn't it? How could all this disappear almost overnight? I guess our heart was telling us that it wouldn't, while our head told us it would.

Foreign exchange was still a large earner for the Tullett group and so, in common with other brokers, we tried to keep our eyes and ears open as to what the banks were up to— as did the Reuters news organisation, which must have been concerned about the implications of automated trading. Reuters, in fact, would launch their own system Dealing 2000, as a direct response.

We didn't have long to wait before the banks, with something of a fanfare, duly launched EBS on a not exactly unsuspecting market. None of us knew how initially to react: would it be significant or a "damp squib"? The early signs were not good and it soon became clear EBS was making a big impression. All markets in spot trading were affected, but the biggest impact was felt in the Far East. For example, in Singapore, where three brokers, who had previously held a third of the market between them, suddenly found this had plummeted to just 3%. This may have been a watershed, but we were all getting wet!

Another factor that caused inertia among brokers was market logic: once EBS was introduced why should brokers pile in and develop their own systems? The market didn't need 100 different systems. It only needed two, just to keep everybody honest!

A main element of success for any business is the ability to anticipate change. Being slow to react to change can be very damaging — not least in the money markets, as we found to our cost with EBS. We knew it was coming, but failed to understand just how successful it would be: at a stroke trading became simpler and more accessible. It had also become more accurate with very few errors now.

While reducing our spot broking employees from 400 globally to around 80, we concentrated on the development of new financial products. We calculated that EBS might damage our business over some five to seven years: in practice, it was five to seven months.

EBS was to more than hold its market share and, now guided by 14 banks, it spread throughout Europe and America and into Asia — the latter through Tokyo Forex's Minex.

We were in difficult times, however our strategy of rapidly developing new products started to take effect and created a cushion for the loss of income. The effects of EBS were such that we could not sustain our losses with the staff levels we had and so we called in our human resources team. Those spot forex staff with something of an academic background were retrained for new products, while others simply had to go.

As well as getting to grips with the arrival of EBS, and the consequent fall-out in spot forex business and the jobs cuts that followed, we also had to cope with launch of the Minex automated deal-matching system, the brainchild of Tokyo Forex and geared to the Asian markets. At the Tullett conference in Spain, Ken Anagita had revealed that initial development costs were $25m. This meant that, as partners, Tulletts suddenly had a balance sheet liability of around $8m — a large and unexpected sum for us at that point.

However, this couldn't have come at a worse moment for Tulletts. Anxious to recoup market share and move forward, we had already warned shareholders not to expect profits. Despite this, we had to take part of the Minex costs on the chin, as a result of our cross shareholding. Minex was eventually to show Ken was right and underlined how well he knew the markets. Minex made such an impression that a merger with EBS became inevitable and, after a series of discussions, did so in 1995. Minex owned two-sixteenths of the new operation — running alongside the holding of the 14 banks — which was a key stake for Ken in what was a substantial business.

By this stage, the total bill for the project had risen to over $30m and our balance sheet had deteriorated by millions of dollars. The Tullett board had not known of Ken's plans; we were struggling to develop our own deal-matching systems —

especially for bonds in New York. The whole EBS/Minex project cost us dearly for a short time — but, fortunately, we cut our prices to remain competitive and so maintained a reasonable place in the spot forex market. We had paid a big price and the number of brokers on the forex desk in the UK was slashed from 150 to 25, with similar cuts in New York and Tokyo.

Without doubt, Tulletts' failure to anticipate the success of EBS was a major mistake. Luckily, this mistake did not prove too costly. As it turned out, EBS managed to hold on to its initial market share — but did not have the management to push it too far forward into other financial products. Had this happened, the market would have been a lot different today.

By 1995, EBS should have pushed towards products such as forwards, which would have been the natural next step; this could have been followed by bonds and swaps, though not, at that stage, derivatives. But there was a certain amount of caution among the owners and a feeling, perhaps, that they were making enough money from EBS spot forex, without the need to expand. Brokers, rather belatedly, reacted to EBS automated deal matching and created their own hybrid deal-matching systems in forex forwards and bonds.

Furthermore, the effect of EBS has become more muted over the years. I was always confident that, even from the earliest days of electronic deal-matching, there would be a role for old-style "voice" broking. And, since 1998, we have seen the "hybrid" method — offering the technology of automated deal-matching enhanced by voice — become very popular with clients and there is now, in 2006, a move to reduce the use of voice.

EBS began the rapid decline in spot foreign exchange business for brokers. Meeting this decline, Tulletts re-grouped its business and moved forward in many ways with so many new products, that, by the time I finally left the company in 2004, forex contributed a very small part of Tullett Liberty's profits.

8

THE MARKETS

Although automated dealing turned out to be a defining moment for broking, the upheaval it brought was very much the exception in what was, both before and after, the smooth evolution of the markets. Up to the 1970s, the markets had traded in much the same way as they had since money broking began in London at the turn of the century. For much of that time the character of the markets displayed a seamless thread captured in an observation by H E Evitt on the 1930s' London scene: "It is a cobweb of telephone wires and peopled only by disembodied voices — it has no meeting place or physical existence."

In the 1920s and 30s foreign exchange was a modest business and remained a "free for all" market despite repeated attempts to regulate both the banking and broking sides. Up to the outbreak of the Second World War there were 32 broking houses in the City. Obviously, 1945 saw a radically-altered world economy and financial dealings took a while to get back on their feet again. In the 1950s mergers, inspired by the Bank of England, saw the number of brokers reduced to 12 as the markets emerged from their wartime hibernation. In those days brokers were allocated currencies and, if they wanted to expand their product base, needed to get the authority of the Bank of England and FEBA.

In the 50s brokers were listed by the Bank, a system that enabled them to operate by becoming members of FEBA. There were three advisory bodies for the market: FEBA represented the brokers, while the Foreign Exchange Committee represented the banks — and these two worked in tandem with the Bank's Joint Standing Committee. The ultimate regulatory body was the Bank, which also supplied the chairman of the JSC.

In this rather bleak post-war world, things only really got moving again when the market began to deal in the newly-floated Canadian dollar and when, shortly after, the Bank made arrangements for the formal re-opening of the foreign exchange market in various currencies against sterling.

For the next seven years exchange arrangements developed through inter-centre dealing in both "spot', where foreign currency changes on the spot: in other words, a market for immediate transfer, and forward "arbitrage", where currencies are bought and sold in simultaneous markets to take advantage of a price difference.

In the 50s and early 60s a simple spot foreign exchange market existed. Because of UK controls at the time, everything was transacted against sterling. You could not trade against the US dollar, although you could against a US/Canadian dollar mix. You could deal in sterling against the dollar in three ways: by mail telegraph, telegraphic transfer or cable. In fact dollar-sterling trades became known as "cable". Different prices existed in mail transfer and telegraphic transfer because it took between two and five days to transfer.

Restrictions were gradually lifted with a limited deregulation of the markets. In 1966 the Bank put its foot on the gas a little more with brokers getting the go-ahead to deal in Eurodollar deposits. This allowed companies to grow in terms of the products they handled and to become more "global" in their reach — a development that was to feature strongly in the years ahead. During this period the Eurocurrency market grew and accelerated further with the move to non-resident convertability. This resulted in an increased turnover for the London broking companies they moved into new products such as short-date forwards.

The profits made by a number of brokers, including Savage & Heath I am pleased to say, were wisely re-invested to satisfy the banks' demands for wider services and greater professionalism. This provided a solid foundation for these brokers to expand their global footprint and client base in later years.

Up to this point, banks in London dealing in foreign exchange could only use brokers who belonged to FEBA, but some banks were dealing with non-members for deposits. This created something of a "little local difficulty" which only began to be resolved in 1967 when it was formally agreed, through what became known as the "Stirling letter", that there should be three types of broker: those operating in foreign exchange; those in sterling deposits in London; and those in currency deposits abroad.

But these arrangements were soon to be put to the test. For a start, with the Eurodeposit markets becoming more competitive, the banks became upset at the rate of 1/32% brokerage. Then there were continuous disagreements over the inclusion of new association members, which we ourselves were to experience in 1971.

Finally, problems intensified when the fast rate of growth in the late 1960s and 70s, plus the development of the inter-bank sterling markets, brought about the need for more and more skills to service these markets. After further discussions, the deposit brokerage rate dropped to .025% and this later became

.020% either side and, together with the current scale for foreign exchange, lasted five years.

At this point, the British clearing banks began to lose their competitive edge because 8% of their deposits in any currency had to be held at the Bank of England. So much so, that by 1960 the banks had less than 10% of the Eurodollar market, the rest being swallowed up by the US banks and the overseas arms of British banks. Exchange controls, as an instrument of government policy, were holding back the City and brought about discussions with the Bank. The government, as it did on many occasions over the 60s and 70s, sought to protect the pound. It could also understand that the City would earn more if institutions lent to foreigners, but was worried about any large outflow of capital in the short term.

The Bank won some small victories — with an easing of exchange control regulations — but the government, through the Bank, was still unsure whether to let the Eurodollar market expand. What the politicians were soon to discover, though, was that London was to become a Eurodollar deposit stronghold regardless of the strength of the pound.

In the 60s a series of major events brought about the explosion of the Eurodollar market. In the first place, the collapse of the post-war Breton Woods agreement which had established a post-war international monetary system of convertible currencies, fixed exchange rates and free trade led to the devaluation of sterling, followed soon after by adjustments to the franc and the deutschmark. On the international stage, the two Arab-Israeli wars in 1967 and 1973 led to a doubling of world oil prices and the deepening war in Vietnam turned the dollar into a deficit situation for the first time.

Post-war British governments had traditionally feared that trends in the money market could lead to funds leaving the country, weakening our deposits and, so, the pound. What the

Bank of England came to see was that the Eurodollar market had a dynamic of its own which had created a very important business that would not crumble. It was based on a "new efficiency" through which lenders and borrowers of funds got together with fewer intermediaries, leading to lower charges and cost savings.

A key year in the development of the Eurodollar was 1963 when London's first foreign currency loan was arranged by the City to fund an Italian motorways project. The deal reflected the growing confidence in the City and it was soon poised for a rapid expansion as US capital became isolated with Washington announcing tax measures and credit controls to protect the balance of payments.

Even so, there were still voices that feared the Eurodollar revolution would explode. They worried what would happen if lenders couldn't get their money back. Despite this, by the mid-60s, London was becoming as much a centre for the dollar, as for sterling. The Eurodollar boom was central to the new type of business that was making the City a very different place.

What we were now seeing was a hunger for capital. The decade's repeated currency instability plus the break-up of Breton Woods meant that the City was uniquely placed to exploit this growing demand, because of its time zone advantage, its critical mass of skills and the fact that it was operating with little, if any, interference from the authorities.

By 1965, four markets were running in "parallel" to the traditional money or discount market. And the Eurodollar was the biggest by far of these parallel markets, which, at this time, expanded as a result of the London-based US banks. This was largely money being sent back to the US for investment by corporations and public bodies. London's second parallel market was a wholesale banking market — the inter-bank market in Eurodollar and sterling deposits — in which the main players were the merchant banks, foreign banks and UK banks operating abroad.

The late 60s saw continued volatility with balance of payments crises going hand-in-hand with currency instability. During these years I recall two key moments on the foreign exchange markets. By 1967 it was obvious in the City that the Labour government would have to devalue and in one memorable weekend in October, it did so to the tune of 15% amid Prime Minister Harold Wilson's famous pledge to protect the "pound in your pocket".

By 1969 the City's parallel money markets in sterling continued to rise, particularly the inter-bank market in sterling deposits, which was now worth £2,000 million a year. The growth of the inter-bank market was a seminal moment for the City because it encouraged fringe, or secondary, banks to use their resources to take on many profitable lending commitments that the clearing banks, tied by credit ceilings, could not. Within 12 months, 90 largely non-deposit banks were competing aggressively for funds in a largely-unsupervised wholesale banking market. It was a time for strong nerves.

Throughout the 50s and 60s the public school ethos dominated the markets. But, while the "old school tie" and family connections still dominated the upper echelons of the City, the end of the 60s numbered their days. They would be found out by the new business challenges of the 70s and 80s and moved sideways through organisations and into administration. The market lost much of its "personality" broker feel and the general light-heartedness that went with it. A new order took its place and the markets became a far more serious place.

The 30 years up to the Millennium saw market changes, in terms of product development and related broker skills, that represented a well-nigh perfect piece of evolution. As we moved into new products, companies trained their staffs to provide them the necessary skill sets to match. Then, as the products became more sophisticated, broking houses took to recruiting an ever-more-educated workforce to match the standards set by our clients and to get to grips with the increasing mathematical complexity of the products.

Most brokers could see about five years ahead and would plan accordingly. The 70s proved to be a decade of learning and development in the money markets: this was the decade that put in place the foundations of today's market. Most brokers had the same concerns: how to manage the market's direction and putting in place an overseas network.

In 1970 banks had finally been permitted to deal directly between themselves and through overseas brokers, while UK brokers — of which there were 12 "voice" brokers — were allowed to deal with overseas banks and correspondent broking companies (apart from New York where we had to wait until 1974) outside the UK. London brokers realised how important this was: their subsequent global coverage and investment in the major financial centres has made them a dominant force in the global broking market.

Sterling came into its own in the 70s and Tulletts had its own sterling deposits section along with deposits on all other currencies. We also set up a team committed to look at all-round arbitrage possibilities. The next 10 years would see a growth in the spot and forward foreign exchange, Eurodollar and sterling deposit markets. Simple arbitrage opportunities existed between these products. Over these years the futures market in Chicago would evolve from commodity-based products to include financial futures.

The early 70s saw currency volatility and the EEC attempted to deal with this by launching its first attempt at harmonising exchange rates. The mechanism adopted — the so-called "Snake in the Tunnel" — saw participating governments required to

confine the fluctuations of their currencies within a range of +/-
1% against each other. The value of the group of currencies (the
snake) had also to be maintained within a range of +/-2.25%
against the US dollar (the tunnel).

In January 1973, Britain, Denmark and Ireland joined the
EEC and in October, the pressure on those currencies, already
struggling to hold their values within the snake, intensified as a
result of the Arab oil embargo imposed following the outbreak of
war between Israel and its neighbours, Egypt and Syria.

The embargos were imposed by Arab oil-producing nations
on America and western European nations who were supporting
the Israelis, and as a result oil prices quadrupled over the
following six months. Over the next two years most participating
currencies were forced out of the snake, eventually leaving only
West Germany, the Benelux countries and Denmark within the
mechanism.

Back in London, the money markets were cleaning up their
act. The final version of the "Stirling letter" was drawn up in 1973
and re-named the "O'Brien letter". (Most banks, and later
members of the Foreign Exchange Committee, signed up.) This
was ratified by the 1973 Fair Trade Act and became the markets'
official document. The agreement sought to bring about a clean,
disciplined market that would set the standard for the rest of the
world. Within it, banks not having the necessary capital or
expertise would not be allowed to operate in London; neither
would brokers with "principal" connections over 10%. Brokers
offering an all-round service were welcomed within the
framework.

The markets were now moving at quite a pace and a
Euromoney survey in 1978 showed that the City was earning
£1.7bn net surplus in foreign exchange; that foreign income had
doubled over two years; that it had more foreign banks than
other financial centres; and that it had more US banks than in

New York. An important landmark came in 1979 when the Banking Act brought in a two-tier system for the markets: authorised banks and licensed deposit takers.

At about his time, there was another landmark event for the markets when the so-called "Sarabex affair" broke. Sarabex, a Frankfurt-based foreign exchange and money broker, had complained to the EEC about restrictive practices. Eventually, the Bank of England relented and Sarabex was admitted to London and to FEBA. The Sarabex episode had revealed how the City was still a cluster of largely self-regulating closed shops. Ten forex broking firms which comprised FEBA, had had a cushioned existence because of:

1. The Bank of England's opposition to brokers being taken over by banks; up to 10% was OK, although there was a small number of companies which welcomed this approach;
2. The Bank's opposition to banks dealing directly with each other in London in foreign exchange; and
3. The fact that banks (members of British Bankers' Association) preferred members of FEBA to conduct their forex and deposit business

These years provided pointers to the fact that the 80s would be a special decade for the City. To start with, there was an irresistible rise of the world's financial markets. For example, the Eurocurrency markets showed that national borders could not prevent the spread of knowledge, ideas or financial data.

The UK financial system was no longer insulated against external financial flows. There was much greater integration between the UK and other financial markets. For 20 years there had, in effect, been two "City's": one, a free-wheeling unregulated Eurocurrency and Forex markets; and the other, a sterling-based, cartel-run domestic market, based on the Stock Exchange.

But with transactions across the markets there was no economic logic for the continuation of this divide. Up to the 70s, the market had been largely spot and forward foreign exchange and Eurodollars and confined, more importantly, to a single centre — that is to say, brokers could not transact business outside their domestic market. This restriction, which meant an imperfect market with no centralised price, was generally imposed by our clients. This situation collapsed in the early 70s and the more adventurous brokers, such as ourselves, invested their profits and expanded their operations into major financial centres throughout the world. Until then, London traders had dealt directly between themselves or through small local broking operations in other centres. New York eventually opened up in 1974.

The London brokers not only incorporated offices in other major centres, but also visited traders outside major centres and installed direct lines to those they felt would be market users. The City had the infrastructure, skills and management (who were not risk averse) to take advantage of the business the brokers brought to London.

The scenario became self-perpetuating: the London brokers met the demands of the London traders with new clients and, a little later, innovative products, subsequently taking the liquidity and new products to their overseas offices which, in turn, expanded their products and client base.

The 1980s saw an explosion of products. By then, spot, forward and Eurodollar trading had been joined in the markets by swaps, options, bonds and derivatives. More recently, credit derivatives and energy futures emerged. All these products evolved naturally out of each other.

In the 80s, senior brokers in each company probably had 10

clients — five large and five medium-sized. Using the open line system, the broker spoke to all clients at the same time, receiving the prices through the loudspeaker. The broker received his orders through this dedicated line and loudspeaker. Usually, the broker recognised the dealer's voice, but if he didn't the line had a voice-activated light to ensure confidentiality. At the same time, codes or cards, containing the names of clients, would be used to pass the name of the buyer or seller. This also ensured confidentiality.

By the mid-80s, major brokers had staff of around 500 in London. Since the 60s London brokers had expanded into areas they believed would be key to a global operation. In September 1982 a new market came to London in the shape of the LIFFE (London International Financial Futures Exchange) to deal in currency and interest rate futures contracts. A financial futures contract is an agreement to buy or sell a standard quantity of a specific financial instrument at a future date at a price agreed between the two parties through "open outcry" on the floor of an organised exchange. Buyers and sellers are under obligation, not to each other, but to the clearing house. Financial futures can be used for hedging — used to reduce the risk of loss through adverse price movements in interest and currency rates — and speculation.

Orders from clients were collected in the traditional manner and transmitted direct to our booth on the floor of the LIFFE — these orders were then passed to the pit with hand signals updating the prices and telling the booth when a deal was completed. London money brokers were not prevented from dealing with commercial companies but largely restricted this activity to the deposit and futures operations.

With the arrival of the 1980s, computers were to the change the face of broking. The survivors in such a competitive arena were likely to be those with quality technology and service: one must go with the other to stay in the race. By the end of that decade I viewed the role of the broker as an equal partnership with the principals working for an overall improvement in the market. The market developed slowly after the war and the major changes only came about after extensive discussions between the Bank of England, FEC and the Brokers' Association. The Association had its own rules and regulations and only twice over 30-odd years, had to penalise a member for infringing its code of conduct. I never believed the Association should have the power to penalise its members. However, my view was largely ignored.

The partnership between the banks, brokers and Bank of England was largely responsible for the reputation that the London market had gained by the 80s. This partnership also gave the brokers the confidence to expand their operations worldwide. Such a growth brought new business to London and the dealers responded with competitive prices. In fact, the large majority of global brokers were either owned or were partners of UK companies.

Brokers realised that they had a responsibility to continually improve their service while maintaining commissions at a fair level. It was essential that brokers kept pace with technology to help them achieve these ends. As ever, the fundamental in broking was to provide a quality product at the right time at a competitive price. The offer of zero brokerage begged two questions: would the broker be able to give the dealer the service required and would the dealer see the business within his price? This would lead to brokers only being able to make money from position taking (which was forbidden). This would subsequently lead to the opening of a "Pandora's Box" of a principal taking a credit rating on any broker operating in this way, which raised issues about the potential undermining of credibility and integrity in the market.

Another issue was "open-line broking" which improved broker service and cut costs, but dealers felt it was at the expense of confidentiality and too high a price to pay. Brokers needed to investigate how to improve service with greater confidentiality. In my view, lack of confidentiality was not actually a major issue despite the occasional errors. However, with deals being transacted in a fast-moving market, the information was immediately history.

The 80s saw the development of the "screen" system of pricing. But efficient broking required an advanced screen system plus quality brokers and the quality of the voice broker remained a vital ingredient. The screen broking method is an obvious one for traded instruments which are identifiable, such as UK gilts. The trick was to adapt screen broking for other markets.

Elsewhere at this time, a decision by Bank of England to halt the merger of Exco and Morgan Grenfell — because of the O'Brien letter restriction of "connection with principals" — caused controversy. Under this clause, principals could only own a certain percentage of a member of the FEBA. Both sides in the merger were not aware of any conflict of interest that might have lost them lines of business. But the general feeling in the market was that the ruling was discriminatory and that any decision about conflict of interest should have been up to the two companies.

As the 80s drew to a close there were two possible strains on the traditional "partnership" between brokers and dealers. Corporate volume traders requested a broker in currency deposits and foreign exchange. Brokers needed this to improve volumes and, thus, their service and to help lower costs. Also brokers were becoming more selective — mainly through their company marketing team — regarding installing lines. All lines were now being based on business potential.

Into the 1990s the products became ever more sophisticated with option contracts available on all of them. Swaps had a serious role to play and there was arbitrage across all asset classes — at Tulletts, we had a team which looked at arbitrage possibilities for all aspects of our broking business. Approaching the Millennium, a different style of broking emerged through credit derivatives which required complex documentation. The evolution of markets continued and the money brokers took advantage of the emergence of commodities and energy products such as oil and weather futures, emission controls etc.

Another important development at this time was the Bank of England handing over City regulation to the Financial Services Authority. Broking houses had always worked well with the Bank and self-regulation was the real name of the game for all those years. It had only required a gentle nudge from the Bank on any given issue for brokers to see the error of their ways and fall into line. The advent of the FSA brought greater formality to the relationship and the overall proceedings.

So, these were the main themes in the markets over three decades. What, then, of those who worked in them? The Sarabex affair in 1979 was symbolic of the pressures on the City to change its culture. Set to go were the long lunches, coming in were corporate conglomerates and a more international outlook.

By the late 1970s, the City had become more open and meritocratic as the Old School Tie way of doing things was rapidly being replaced by a hungrier intake into broking of state-educated graduates for whom the sky was the limit in terms of possibilities. The 70s saw the start of a vast earning potential for brokers which became even more marked in the 80s which was a decade of excess with firms making huge profits and brokers earning a lot of money, often via their bonuses. But they paid a price. Spot brokers, for example, were subjected to prolonged pressure and the average working life in this sector was 15 years.

At Tulletts, we always took the view that when spot brokers lost their appetite we retrained them for another less-concentrated area of the business. We also retrained brokers in areas which were declining and moved them to growth sectors,

Forex and deposits trading exists in something of a parallel universe with the derivatives side. While all sides of the broking business require a supreme sales temperament, derivatives are more technical and complex and necessitate a further ingredient that largely requires university-educated individuals.

As to salaries, the markets became a very highly-paid place to earn a living in the 80s and 90s. For the first time, brokers earned more than their dealer clients and the banks were not happy with this. Parity has been restored, however, in recent years. It's still the case that the top 5%-10% of brokers earn high salaries. In general, the younger broker receives a higher percentage of his salary in commission, sometimes over 50%, possibly reducing over the years to 10%, as the older broker prefers stability in his income.

Seen in football terms: 15%-20% of brokers are in the Premier League — the top brokers who run things. They are the dealing board conductors, who probably never become directors, as "titles" are not important to them. The next 20%-25% are in the Championship supporting the "stars" in the Premiership. The First Division is made up of promising trainees and those who are satisfied with their position and salary. They work hard and are important part of the company; the rest — around 15% — drift from firm to firm not accepting any responsibility. The salary gap between the first rank and second ranks is large; the gap between second and third ranks and between third and fourth is a lot narrower.

Even though vast sums could be earned, it wasn't enough for some. I recall trying to recruit a futures trader who I thought was rather special and I was prepared to push the boat out to get him. The interview went well as he told me he found his job boring and wanted a new challenge. Then we got to the salary: he indicated it had to be six figures. I asked for a few minutes to think about it and agreed to his demands: £100,000 it was, then. "Sorry," came the reply, "I already earn £200,000 working for myself from a futures 'room'!"

Recruitment had become a crucial issue in itself. Over the years, Tulletts recruited extensively outside the market and trained new staff. Trainees were on a six-month probationary period to give them a broad view of the City, the money markets and our company. After that, those staying on were allocated a local director for the next six months. This proved a successful formula. Throughout the 80s Tulletts reacted to client needs by matching brokers to dealers in terms of background and temperament.

We also went for brokers who were keen on sport and team games – because broking is a team game. The dealing room and the money market are no places for a loner, no places to be on your own: isolated brokers are unproductive for firms because they are unlikely to make serious money and dangerous for firms because they may be being secretive and operating on the edge of legality.

By the mid-80s, and with business booming, brokers were recruiting in ever increasing numbers. But, as broking gained a higher public profile, more and more people wanted to join the industry and Tulletts was receiving 100 unsolicited letters a week from wannabe brokers. This was in stark contrast to the 60s and 70s when Larry Woolman at Savage & Heath and, later, Alan Styant at Tullett & Riley had interviews without even knowing what money broking was!

In another twist to the jobs merry-go-round, FEBA tried to get involved by calling on members not to poach staff from each other. This idea was given short shrift. How can you tell people where they should work? A case of the weak brokers in FEBA trying to tell their strong counterparts what to do and, of course, this was never going to work.

In general terms, money broking moved towards the Millennium in good heart having absorbed new products, Big Bang and wider markets. The biggest human concern in the City in the 90s was the twin threat of drugs and corruption. I thought a tougher line by senior management in both brokers and dealers was needed to cope with the irresponsible behaviour of a minority in the City at night and at weekends.

I think we had fewer problems at Tulletts than did most brokers. We suspected that the few brokers taking drugs were snorting cocaine in bars at night and using cannabis at the weekend. To combat this, we operated random testing and if tests proved positive, the broker concerned had six weeks to go away and receive treatment under the company's healthcare scheme — at the end of which we expected them to be clean. If they were then found to be taking drugs they were out. We only had four cases over all the years, as a result of which only one employee was dismissed. A victory for a firm-but-fair policy.

As for corruption, this was usually associated with freely negotiable brokerage. But I was confident a tough line would be taken if it ever reared its head in London.

This then has been the markets to date: where do they go from here? To start with, there is scope for all-round growth and for new product development. EBS is moving down a retail route (and, as I write, is the subject of a takeover bid by ICAP), but Tullett Prebon is unlikely to follow this strategy. The argument against the retail route is that by going down that road you are taking the banks' clients — and what is there then left for the banks?

Globally, India and China are coming on stream. While China is the flavour of the month and a popular bet with investors, my hunch is India. I think it will do better because, unlike China, it has a legal and accounting system that, as a result of our colonial past, is understood in Britain. On the other hand, both countries are massive "gamblers" — so that bodes well.

Elsewhere, Dubai is looking to be a significant player with the opening of the Dubai International Financial Centre and to do so it needs to attract Middle Eastern money away from London and New York. Bahrain and Qatar, meanwhile, are pushing for the big time by building their own financial cities.

In terms of products, there is still plenty of scope for adding to the existing 40 or so products in the marketplace — quite a contrast to the "spot only" single product days of the 1950s. Credit derivatives will continue to play a major role. Through credit derivatives, investors can quickly get out of currencies they no longer wish to be in.

I also see a number of other developments. Tullett Prebon runs a hybrid system — a mix of automated deal-matching with voice back-up. I see the hybrid system continuing, but involving fewer people. And I also expect some form of back-up and helpline to remain. As for profitability, I anticipate the margins in automated deal-matching are likely to tighten, with some clients still preferring to deal in voice and being prepared to pay more for this back-up.

Second, I believe current dealing systems will go on to the internet. This way, we will be dealing with companies around the world on one system. In turn, that will see a hybrid system developing in each major financial centre with a sales force dealing with the rest of the world. Following on from that, I don't think we will have more human resource involved in existing products. But, by contrast, when new products — similar to credit derivatives — come on line then human resource will, initially, have a large part to play.

The markets will also become more technical. When figures

are released or announcements made in any leading country, teams of economists are picking them up, analysing them and appraising the information for the market participants. We all know about conventional spread betting involving gambles in all forms of sport and politics and the like. But the idea of spread betting in financial products fascinates me: with my history in the money markets I am intrigued by the possibility of trading financial products by these other methods and that's where a lot of my future business interests will be concentrated.

9
THE MANAGEMENT

It's one thing to have theories about management, whether your own or anyone else's. It's quite another to be able to put them into practice successfully and, in so doing, improve the business health of your company and the corporate life of its staff. There's nothing magical about it. You can't just turn up and sprinkle fairy dust over an organisation and make it work.

Management is a fine blend of nurture and nature: nurture, in terms of what you learn; and nature, in terms of your instinct. Also, I think any management approach should start out with a set of business principles. Mine have been honed over the whole of my career and have come from sources both large and small and have been important building blocks in my management style.

The first, and possibly the best, piece of advice I ever received came from Jack Liddel, one of ANZ's top traders, who said to me as I left the company: "Remember, Derek, always put ethics before profit." The other important comment came from Bernard Searle who confided: "When you're trading, don't worry about the rate, keep the principle intact!" What he meant, was that you should ensure that whoever you lend to can repay you when the loan matures.

Being in business isn't all about being hard-nosed, it's about having principles. I've carried principles with me throughout my career and have always turned to them, ultimately. In business, you certainly need to be innovative. In business, there are times when you need to have sharp elbows. In business, you need to be competitive. But all business must be conducted within certain rules: there must be an ethical line beyond which you cannot go.

Now, I know there's an old joke: "Why is 'ethics' an optional course at Harvard?"

But while ethics may be optional at Harvard, it's not in the City: ethics have guided me through good times and bad in business. While it's easy to have principles when things are going well, it's not so easy when the tricky moments arise — such as the emergence of drugs in London and New York and corruption elsewhere in Europe during the 1980s and 90s.

I have been firmly against drugs throughout my career during which, at one stage, drug taking became a problem. And as the drug problem spread, the Tullett board — after much discussion and heart searching — decide it had to act to combat it by introducing random drugs testing.

A number of influences have informed my approach to management. On a broad canvas, National Service certainly offered me a crucial lesson in man management: how to handle errors. I'm pretty relaxed about most things. If someone makes a small error, I actually don't mind. Simple mistakes don't bother me; however, major mistakes do and in business you have to react. I try to explain to everybody that leadership in these situations is about taking tough decisions — particularly when it involves people you like, people you are friendly with. That is very tricky, but very necessary.

And if there was one consistent failing at Tulletts down the years it was the inability of managers to take tough decisions with staff they regarded as friends. They wanted to be liked rather than be effective. What they couldn't see is that managers will be liked if they do their job properly and effectively.

What other influences did I come under? Well, books on management had a definite, if limited, impact. And even when we became bigger and certain new issues arose, I resisted the temptation to reach for the management books — or turn to any so-called management gurus — in search of ways to deal with them. I never tried to apply any management theory that was not relevant to the business in which we were engaged. Books on management can offer a foundation of thought, but in companies like Tulletts, management has to be unique to the needs of that particular business. You can't take a management that's been successful in one sphere and transplant it elsewhere and expect the same outcome.

What conclusions have I come to then about good management? Generally speaking, quality management should not be cyclical, it should be on-going and should have a continuity of personnel and outlook. This, in turn, can be achieved in a number of ways, which I would place under the headings: communication, flexibility, attitude/approach and decision-making.

Obviously, good communication between management and staff is crucial and is usually based on sound structures within the company. What does good communication amount to? At the simplest level, a manager who sorts out a problem quickly and efficiently, may be viewed as a good operator. The real communicator, in my opinion, is the manager who examines why the problem arose in the first place and sets about preventing it happening again. Dealing with the symptoms is one thing, removing the cause is another.

Rooting out the cause of a problem can be achieved in a number of ways. The best way is to consult those responsible for existing methods. It is essential for all concerned to analyse thoroughly the existing methodology. The difficulty for management arises in the deliberations that have to take place before a solution can be arrived at. If the basics are correct, then there is every reason to adopt a "layer" solution, which simply fits another level to an existing sound structure. But it's no solution to "layer" on to an inefficient system. If inefficiency is the problem, then it's time to devise a new system.

It is also important not to fall into the trap of believing that in difficult times a change of strategy will be the remedy. All too often a company struggles not because the strategy is incorrect, but, rather, because the strategy is not being implemented correctly. Senior management demand that information and ideas percolate up through the management structure. However, they must also insist that the resulting strategy is passed down — making strategy and flexibility the responsibility of everybody in the company. As the management guru of the 80s, Robert Heller, once observed: "You don't have to be senior to have senior ideas."

If the existing corporate culture and management attitudes do not permit the free flow of ideas and strategy in an organisation, then the time has come for a change of culture and management.

Information flow and opinions are another key element in good communication. And the starting point for good information flow is that each member of staff is regarded as important as the other and that everyone should be pro-active in expressing their opinions.

Flexibility is an important feature of management's never-ending quest for greater efficiency. How often do we here the refrain: "But it's always been done this way" Just because it's always been done in a certain way does not mean it is the most efficient way to do it! It merely emphasises a mistrust of change, which must be overcome. It is important to be flexible and to realise that a change of fundamentals is often essential for progress and for a continued ability to compete at the highest level. A company must have the ability to embrace change and move away from prepared positions, and to do this it must always build in a bit of "wriggle room" to its plans.

As I told a Tullett planning conference in Marbella in the summer of 1991: "In this fast moving and fiercely competitive market, the solutions of last year are almost certainly not appropriate for the future. It would be effortless for management to allow our group to drift, only responding to market events and to the natural evolution of the market. But this cannot be our sole perception of the future if we are determined to achieve our goal."

A business progresses on vision and on judgment about probabilities, not certainties; and, in planning for a future full of uncertainties, it is important to retain flexibility. New developments can, on occasions, surprise an organisation. However, these developments must not be ignored — otherwise management gets locked into a non-flexible approach. By reacting to new developments with greater alacrity than your competitors, potentially tricky new developments can be turned into opportunities.

New developments or "surprises" create moments of business instability which require instant reaction and must be resolved before management can continue the less time-sensitive role of achieving its medium and long-term strategy. And as the horizons lengthen, strategies become less detailed — as a result, the long-term view comprises objectives and goals.

So, reacting to surprise developments is very important. Indeed, I would go as far as to say that an over-reliance on planning theory and an under-estimation of the importance of random factors is a recipe for failure. Having said that, planning is, of course, a vital ingredient. For while excessive planning will not reduce unpredictability, competent planning is key for the future to the point that any success achieved without planning is down to good luck and not good management. Flexibility, therefore, is essential.

Decision-making is the next factor in good management. As Tulletts matured as a company, we were able to adopt a cellular approach to organisation; this encouraged decision-making, without varying any parameters, to permeate through the whole company structure. Where this is successful it is a testimony to a correct recruitment process. We were able to adopt the cellular approach because we clearly believed we had the right employees.

Decisions about the day-to-day broking techniques were taken close to the action — so responding to the evolving requirements of dealers. This meant we were reliant on brokers, section managers and directors to react and implement any necessary changes to the dealing culture.

Market signals from desk level were fed upward through various boards, either via minutes or by word of mouth, to the international board who used this to formulate group strategy. Before doing so, the board discussed the ramifications with senior management in all offices. As a result, decisions could be based on consultation: this was management by persuasion, not edict. Having made the decision, it is then sent back through the same route. To some extent, this is a counsel of perfection, implying the time needed to carry out decisions. There were times, of course, when the international board didn't have the luxury of time to consult and had to act quickly.

A further aspect of management is the need to take decisions against an unsettled background. Unpredictability will widen the range of decision options and, as a company's workforce becomes more educated, decision-making can be forced down through the organisation, encouraging developing management to take risk and responsibility.

An integral part of management today, and in the future, will be the ability to demonstrate to junior colleagues the thought process required for future planning and decision-making.

One of the important attributes of a good manager is the power to attract quality people to work in the organisation. However, it is the blending of these quality individuals into a team and the leadership exercised which will influence things in the long-term future. At the same time, management's timidity in their encouragement of decision-making at every level will lead an organisation into mediocrity and subsequent stagnation.

The final element in my theory of management is attitude and approach. Being positive has clear benefits for an organisation, but there is a role for what you might call "negative" thinkers. A note of caution from the negative thinker perhaps triggers more thought about a project and may lead to a different and improved approach. The problem is how to turn the negative thought into a creative outcome or solution to a problem.

And there is even a third group of thinkers, beyond the negative critical and positive creative, who recognise the value of an idea and will debate how the idea can be maximised. Creative and constructive thinking can mean more work and hassle. This is not always the case as many new ideas simplify life.

It is management's role to encourage creativity and constructive thinking from every employee and to provide an environment where they are encouraged to express their ideas. Management has the responsibility to ensure all creative ideas that fit into long-term plans are implemented regardless of the additional work burden this places on them.

A central part of a company's attitude and approach is its ability to be acutely sensitive to its client's needs at all times, which helps it to maintain competitive advantage. But how do you determine client requirements? Every point of contact with clients has to be viewed and utilised as a quality contact. It is the function of all staff to acquire market information and for this information to be made available to senior management.

Responsibility must be forced through the organisation to ensure information and ideas bubble up within it. It is the quality of information and its interpretation that supports senior management in its development of strategy.

If an employee turns out to be wrong for the job is it the fault of the person who hired them? In our industry, the success of individuals is largely determined by the support and assistance of management and colleagues. If we all regard the non-performance of a colleague as our fault we have a good opportunity, through collaboration and never coercion, to improve their performance levels.

We depend on each other's skills to achieve our ambitions. The policy of teamwork will elicit superior performance from adherence and compel senior management to reappraise each team member's performance and potential: money broking cannot afford one weak link and complacency is the enemy of progress.

Well that's the theory, as I see it. But what did I learn from the day-to-day Tullett experience? I think it's fair to say that the late 1980s and early 1990s were not the best management years at Tulletts, while in different ways, the early 1970s and late 1990s were certainly the best.

In the early years our management consisted of a small inner group of colleagues — a critical mass, if you like — all going in the same direction and around which our business was run. Up to that point, any management issues that arose could be sorted out quickly as we were so close to the staff. As we grew this became more difficult — particularly when you bear in mind we employed about 3,000 people around the world.

In the early 80s founding partner David Riley had gone and — although his skills were still available to me as a friend — our management became too self-centred and didn't look far enough outside the boardroom. At that time I tried to expand slightly by introducing a change of direction: but change can be frightening not only to staff — a fact that's very well documented — but to management as well, which is perhaps not so well understood.

During this period our management failed to connect with those under them. They thought it was enough to be in the bar with them after work, whereas they would have been better off sitting down in the office discussing work and any problems that were arising.

A really good spell was the late 1990s and this was down to two things which transformed our ability to manage the business better. The first was to introduce two tiers of management: the board, which set strategy and the executive committee, chaired by the chief executive who also sat on the board, executed the strategy. The strategists and doers!

This worked particularly well under Bruce Collins after he returned to London from Japan in the late 1990s. The situation was as follows. While some matters were reserved for the board — for example, anyone being recruited on a salary package over a certain figure, contracts, budgets etc had to have the board's sanction — the executive committee ran the London operation within their parameters. London had its own management committee and they were represented on the executive committee

Board meetings ran far more smoothly as a result and didn't get bogged down in detailed aspects of IT or finance which, although important, could now be identified in advance, allowing board members to be briefed and giving them the chance to minute their opinions beforehand.

The second smart thing we did was to introduce the three-year strategy/targets and it was amazing how often we hit that target spot on. All the directors knew the markets well and so it proved relatively easy to set and commit to a rolling three-year programme such as ours. Every six months we reviewed the strategy and re-set the three-year time frame. This management structure enabled senior directors to obtain information before making it available to junior management and senior staff.

Another factor which shaped our approach was time. In money broking, we had to make instant decisions; hour by hour, day by day. And many Tullett managers, coming from the hurly burly of the dealing room, took some time to adjust to the idea that they did not have to make snap decisions, that they had the luxury of a few more hours to come to consider what to do, before arriving at a conclusion.

An extra dimension to our management in the broking industry was the fact that we were answerable to authorities such as the Bank of England and, latterly, the FSA, for the decisions individuals took. Bad decisions are usually taken when the managers are absent — witness what futures trader Nick Leeson did and the havoc it wreaked for Barings.

We had to take corporate responsibility on a few occasions for the actions of our staff. On one memorable occasion, and with the help of a dealer, a broker — whose manager was on holiday — was running an unofficial book in Greek drachmas and was doing exceptionally well. However, he was undone when he was overtaken by events (in this case an earthquake) and his spectacular gains turned to spectacular losses — £250,000 in all — and we reported it to the authorities. He didn't come out of it too badly as it was decided it less a case of fraud, and more a case of "Look what I can do on my own!" — for which he had his knuckles rapped. And rightly so.

Summing up, I believe that the single most important thing in management is that everything you do must be done ethically and in the company's interests not yours. Pinning it down, I'd say our best management decisions were opening in New York, where we were way ahead of our rivals, and being the first to have a joint venture in Japan. And, if pushed, our worst decision was probably allowing me to be part of the board of the Belgium company. Oh well, you can't win 'em all!

10

THE FAMILY

This was always going to be a difficult chapter, as it is now proving to be. I have always tried to distinguish my private life from my business career. In writing my memoirs, I now have to face the problem of how much of my private life I should expose. For while my business requires me to be an extrovert, this does not come naturally to someone who is rather shy, and particularly when I am dealing with my private life. Anyway, here goes.

So, while I usually separate my business and private worlds, there are, I think, things — attitudes or approaches if you like, call them what you will — that carry over from one world to the other. To start with, in decision-making I have always tried persuasion rather than edict, and that holds good for both the boardroom and the domestic front. However, in both spheres I am prepared, ultimately, to take the decision I believe to be correct and to stand by it.

Also, I set great store by the ability to relax in the midst of what can be a hectic world whirling around you. During these moments, which are brief — perhaps just five minutes or so — I can blank my mind completely. I am, I suppose you would literally say, "thought-less", or better still, "without thought".

After this short break from thinking, during which I can be wonderfully relaxed, I am then ready to continue working for many hours.

I was reminded of this capacity to "blank out" thoughts, while reading Norman Lebrecht's book "The untold story of Covent Garden". As I had realised the value of "blanking" I assumed that everybody else could do it. Not so, as Lebrecht points out in relating a conversation between the economist Maynard Keynes and his wife, Lydia, a former ballerina.

"What are you thinking about?" Keynes asked.

"Nothing," replied Lydia.

"I wish I could," remarked Keynes sadly.

And that became her gift to him — introducing Keynes to an "out of mind" life that was pure escapism.

What then of life away from the world of business? My family has always been at the centre of my private life. My wider family provided the context for my formative years and my two marriages has produced four sons, with whom I am very close.

Consciously or not, you absorb a lot of your attitudes and approach to life from your family in the very earliest days and I've always admired my parents' happy marriage, which was based on strong values. But in the modern world, with its greater pressures and an ever-changing culture, there is a lighter approach to marriage. All businessmen, particularly those whose companies have a global reach, face many difficult moments in their career trying to juggle work commitment and home life – and, clearly, I was no exception. While as an adult I have been very career minded, I have also valued my family and tried to take them into account in everything I've done. The problem has always been the ability to join up the dots or, as it's called these days, achieving work/life balance.

Although a family man, I have never pursued my family history, as such. I've never wanted to chart my family tree — it's just not in my nature. I tend not to look back, only forward. As a result, I don't know too much about my family background — where they came from and when. My mother's maiden name was Flatman and her family heralded from the Norfolk Broads, hence the name. And somewhat underlining the East Anglian connection, I think that an uncle of mine rose to a senior position in Norwich Union insurance. Elsewhere in my mother's family, I know that her father and brother both died of TB between the wars, while her younger sister died in the sixties.

On my father's side, the Tullett name is difficult to trace back because it's not that common. It's been suggested that it originates from France and came to this country with the Hugenots in East Anglia; the name that's closest is *tuiler*, (tile worker). Be that as it may, I do know that the Tullett name has definite links with Bristol and sea-faring and trade.

As for my own parents, they both came from south London, though the two families did not know each other. I'm not clear how Vera Flatman met Percy Tullett — I can only assume it was at something like a social evening. On marrying, they lived in Dulwich and when I was born, my mother became a full-time housewife, while my father continued to manage his business importing and exporting fruit and vegetables. They moved to Shirley near Croydon and lived there for many years before settling near to me in Keston in the 1980s.

My father had been retired from his business aged 70 and he died of a heart attack in 1992, aged 77. All his life he had been a keen sportsman, having played cricket for Croydon and football for St Albans. He was also an enthusiastic sports watcher and followed my rugby fortunes with great interest, attending matches all over the country. My mother, who died in 2003 aged 92, was, until her latter years, a very enthusiastic gardener and her skills were there for all to see.

My introduction to the opera and classical music came via my mother's younger sister Patricia and her husband Dick Francis, who was an auditor for Crown Agents. Over the years I enjoyed their hospitality and found it easy to relax in their company. When I returned from Malaya in 1955 the flight landed at Cyprus for an overnight stop and, fortunately, Dick and Patricia were based there on a short-term posting for Crown Agents. They met me at the airport for a lightning tour and then on to a sumptuous meal — my first since joining the army.

In 1960 they invited Eileen and I to join them on their summer holiday, touring in their Worsley car — visiting Venice via the Dolomites. This was my first trip to Italy, a wonderful country. Sadly, Patricia died in 1979 at the age of 55, while Dick died in 2003.

As I write, I have one uncle surviving on my father's side. Arthur, who is 95, lives with his wife Maureen in Coulsdon, Surrey and they have three sons. The only other relative I am aware of is my cousin Madeleine, the daughter of my father's eldest brother, who lives in St Albans.

Early family life revolved around many get-togethers — most memorably, those involving my father's three spinster sisters. These maiden aunts of mine — Hilda, Grace and Ruby — were all talented musicians and, at Christmas particularly, we had great musical get-togethers around the piano singing carols, during which the local vicar would often drop in for tea. These occasions were marked by hearty singing, much merriment, paste and jam sandwiches and no alcohol — in other words, a typical Edwardian-style family gathering in the drawing room. All this was great fun for a small boy like me.

Of many other family moments in my childhood, two others stand out, both involving holidays. On a caravan trip to Swanage, Dorset in July 1951, my best friend Ronnie Montague and I shocked my parents by getting up a 2am to listen, bleery eyed, to radio commentary of Randolph Turpin defeating American

Sugar Ray Robinson to win boxing's World Middleweight title. I remember we were so excited because Sugar Ray had only been beaten once in 133 previous fights.

Some years later, when I was 17, I went to see some relatives in Paris. I was staggered by the life they led: they had a super apartment, an expensive car and ate in excellent restaurants. Here was a nation that had been invaded and occupied by Nazi Germany, but things seemed plentiful. Britain, by contrast, though victors in war, knew only austerity. To me, my cousin's lifestyle was nothing short of astonishing — not least, when he showed how adept he was at chatting up the local girls! I recall, too, that during that visit we went to the Cognac plant where I drank wine for the first time. You could only stay there for one hour maximum in the Cognac blending room as the fumes were so great.

Of course, there comes a time in life when you find your wider family dwindling not growing and, I'm afraid to say, the only contact I have with them these days is the occasional wedding and, more regularly, at funerals.

My immediate family has evolved from two marriages and my relationship with Gloria, my partner of six years. I met my first wife, Eileen, in the mid-1950s and we married soon after. She worked for an insurance company in the City and her father was a senior figure with Guinness Mahon who had offices almost next door to my early Savage & Heath office, above the Jamaica Inn.

During the 1960s we had two sons, Glenn and Neil — unusually, both names of astronauts from the American space programme — and we enjoyed some good family times in our first single-storey home in Kenley, Surrey. That house looked out across the Caterham Valley to Riddlesdown, just south of Croydon. I remember reading that at one time, Riddlesdown was a very popular holiday spot for people living in the East

End, who flocked to the area to pick fruit in the orchards.

I have never regarded myself as a DIY expert and my first attempt persuaded me never to try it again! On that one and only occasion, I installed two wall lights in the hallway, which appeared to work perfectly well until a visitor rang the front door bell and this immediately blew the lights!

In 1960 we moved from Kenley to a two-storey house in West Wickham. At West Wickham we socialised. Eileen's family occasionally dropped by as we got together to play cards — solo whist, I recall — which was a simple, somewhat unsophisticated, and yet immensely enjoyable, entertainment, typical of the times. Eileen's father was another keen gardener and kept a fine allotment in Addiscombe near Croydon. But domestic problems were to build up and Eileen and I divorced in 1967 and, though going our separate ways, we have remained on good terms since.

I met Anita, who was to be my second wife, while we were colleagues at Savage & Heath and, as so often happens, a close working relationship developed into something more. The eroticism of shared endeavour I believe they call it; or, as the journalist Katherine Whitehorn, once cleverly observed: "Nothing propinqs like propinquity!"

At Savage & Heath, Anita worked in the "back office" team, dealing with the firm's admin. Although she was well paid, her role was not challenging and she did not feel she had a career there. After thinking about her future for some time — and considering a job with British Airways — she jumped at the chance to join the newly-formed Tullett & Riley in 1971, believing a start-up operation would offer more challenge and excitement.

Anita worked in the accounts department at Tullett & Riley and, after our relationship developed, she went to New York with me in 1972 as the company set up operations there. In fact, Anita got involved in most, if not all, of our office start-ups around the world. On our return from New York, we married and Anita worked on in London until our first son, Jonathan, was born in 1973. Our second son, Kevin was born two years later.

My four sons — Glenn, Neil, Jonathan and Kevin — are all different in temperament, outlook and choice of career. But, despite being step-brothers, they all get on well; the older boys have always made the younger two welcome and they are great friends. I am tremendously proud of each of them and we get together a fair amount in different ways throughout the year and the one thing that unites all these occasions is that they treat me like a friend, rather than a father.

The boys have provided that constant thread in my family life and have acted as a unifying factor amid much change over the years. I am in touch with each of them every week and we usually find time to meet up as a family throughout the year.

I recall lots of happy family times, often when I was able to blend business and pleasure by having Anita and the boys with me like we did in Singapore in 1979, and at the opening of our offices in Bahrain and Abu Dhabi. This way, the boys certainly got to see the world while they were young. In both Bahrain and Abu Dhabi, we had apartments next to the office. Every week, I said: "I am not going to answer the office telephone after 7pm." And every week I answered the office telephone 24 hours a day.

Neil recalls an early family holiday in Italy when we were involved in a multi-car pile-up on the way to sightseeing at Pompeii. There was a massive shunt among the cars and all the traffic stopped. Our hire car was hit and we somehow managed to send for another. The man delivering it burst into tears when he saw the damage!

On another trip to see the "Lions of Longleat", I drove at some speed in my Lotus through the monkey enclosure and Glenn said: "Look dad, there's a monkey. Can we slow down?"

"No" came the firm reply. At which point, I accelerated even harder, fearing the monkeys might damage the car's fibreglass body.

After the New York office opened, the boys came to stay for six weeks. There were the usual trips to Palasades Park, Niagra Falls and even to a summer camp. Neil remembers that at one point I overslept and tried to make up time by driving from our rented house in Fairlawns into Manhattan, only to find downtown New York closed off for a "tickertape welcome" for the US astronauts!

When Neil was 13 he and Glenn were joined by Jonathan and Kevin for a trip to Singapore. Kevin was learning to read and had left his "Janet and John" book behind. We hunted high and low but could not find a replacement in Singapore, so had to have one couriered from London at three times the cost of the book!

There was a visit to Abu Dhabi in 1975 where we stayed at the Hilton, but the trip I remember most came in 1979 when all the boys came on a business trip to Bahrain around Christmas time. While the family flew Concorde, the rest of the office team went by 747 and arrived sooner as our supersonic jet experienced technical problems.

On that trip, Neil and Glenn slept in the flat attached to the office and at one stage they showed Jonathan and Kevin the splendours of the local beach without explaining the "quicksand" nature of it — which was why there was no-one on it except for us! In fact, there was one scary moment when Neil and Glenn picked up their younger brothers only to sink further into the sand with the greater weight. Luckily, we managed to rescue them.

I had bought my current home at Keston Park near Orpington in 1971 (more of which later) and Anita, the boys and myself had many happy years here, particularly after we had a swimming pool built in the garden. While it enabled Jonathan and Kevin to invite friends to swim, it also added to my frustration of keeping the pool clean. In our garden there are seven pine trees and their needles would block the filters and required much cleaning.

We also had enjoyable family holidays at our house near Cannes which we bought in 1990. In the south of France we enjoyed water-skiing behind our own boat, using the gymnasium and playing squash. Close by was a health club, owned by Clive and Debbie Stokes, with squash courts and we were all enthusiastic players. Sadly, I was now losing out at squash to my sons. And talking of squash, membership of the Bromley Town Squash And Fitness Club has helped us to build a large circle of friends.

Down the years the boys also spent time with their grandparents. I recall one holiday that involved the wider family, when Anita and I and the boys were joined by my parents in Cyprus. When my parents lived at Ash Tree Way they gave each of the boys a present when they came to visit. My parents also liked to get involved and help out where they could. My father, for example, took it upon himself to drive the boys down to the family house at Bexhill where they had some peace and isolation in which to revise for their exams. This became something of a family tradition. Not that it did Neil that much good. Having discovered a nearby public callbox that didn't seem to need coins, he recalls spending one whole weekend on the phone to his girlfriend.

Meanwhile, the boys' great grandmother Nell lived in Brighton with her sister Mel and the boys visited them from time to time, which brought about some adventures. Like the day Neil was on his way there when the water pump went on his car stranding him on the M23. I have great memories of Grandma Edith who died just short of her 100th birthday.

I also had an antiques dealer second cousin who had a large

property in Shoreham, Sussex, the scene of some large family get-togethers in summer. Such gatherings involved the odd drama or two — such as the time Neil fell 10 feet over a wall during a game of "hide and seek".

Education and sport have always been inextricably linked for the Tullett family. Glenn, who was born in February 1961 in Redhill, Surrey, had a successful academic and sports career — particularly athletics and rugby — at both Greenhayes and Whitgift. I was disappointed, though, that he didn't go to university,

Neil also went to Greenhayes, after which he went on to Alleyn's School and had many friends in the Dulwich area. Neil was reasonably academic but enjoyed sport more. Glenn's friends — because of going to school in Croydon —tended to be in the Surrey area. Before that, Glenn and Neil played rugby together at Greenhayes and both of them recall that after practice each Saturday morning during the season, they went to a restaurant for lunch. With Neil further claiming that he had the same meal each Saturday for five years!

Jonathan was educated at St David's College, West Wickham and later went on to Dulwich College but never settled there, so ending up at my alma mater, Whitgift. From there, at the age of 18, he went on an athletics scholarship to Iowa University in August 1991. With my regular absences abroad, Jonathan and his brother Kevin had become a source of great comfort to Anita and, so, Jonathan's decision to go to America proved an enormous wrench for her. But she put her personal feelings to one side as she enthusiastically helped him prepare for his new life and she and Kevin travelled with him to Iowa for the start of term.

Anita told me later that as all the American students arrived in big cars chock full of equipment and creature comforts — such as, TVs, stereos and fridges — Jonathan turned up with just one suitcase full of clothes! Anyhow, according to Anita, his room was "like a palace" and she and Kevin visited him several times a year over the four years he as there and, indeed, Kevin spent his "gap year" at Iowa University as a student.

Jonathan was an all-round sportsman and gained county caps not only in athletics, but also in rugby, squash, swimming and water polo. But he settled on athletics and chose Iowa because of its reputation for top-class sports facilities — it was one of America's Top Ten sports universities — and, while doing his Ancient Civilisation and Greek philosophy degree, was able to develop his hurdling and was a regular team member. He settled in very quickly and thoroughly enjoyed Iowa. On graduating in 1995, he moved to the Chicago Business School and took a masters degree in quantum mathematics.

After this achievement, and much to our surprise, Jonathan returned to Britain. He had clearly entertained thoughts of making a career out of athletics, but he is a realist and saw that he wasn't quite good enough — that is, not in Britain's top three — to be a professional athlete. He took the view that he had committed a lot of time to athletics and had enjoyed it, but now it was time to move on.

Like Jonathan before him, Kevin went to St David's and Whitgift where he also proved a keen sportsman with rugby, squash, swimming and water polo proving to be his games of choice.

As a family we have played a lot of squash together, but in more recent years, we have turned more to skiing. Jonathan and Kevin , having learned at a young age, have become excellent skiers and took pleasure in commenting on our style while managing to ski backwards themselves!

Cars have always been important to the Tullett men and when the boys entered their teens there was some keen anticipation about taking to the road. But there were a few things to bear in mind. By the time Glenn was 15 all his school friends had 50cc bikes — however, I refused to let him have one after hearing that a friend's son was killed riding a moped. Instead, I promised him that if he forewent a bike, I would buy him a car on his 17th birthday. When that day arrived I delivered on my promise in the shape of a nifty little Hillman Imp which I bought for £50 from my secretary. The engine needed rebuilding — some cylinders had rusted up — but it did a good job in doubling up as Glenn's first car and later I raced in it.

Neil's first car was a Fiat, which he crashed early on. Despite my earlier concerns about mopeds, Jonathan managed to get himself a 500cc motorcycle and I recall seeing him struggling up a hill only to be overtaken by a bus!

One of the trickiest family moments for Kevin, though not for me, involved one of my much-loved cars. My Lotus's, and subsequently Ferraris and a Bentley, were always blocking the driveway at Keston and probably put temptation in the path of a young boy, with almost predictable results. At 19, Kevin was out in my Lotus Excel when he crashed and wrote it off. Fearing my wrath, he only felt able to call me about it after talking to Jonathan about it. But, he needn't have worried, I was only concerned that he was not injured. As much as I may enjoy my cars, I love my sons.

My sons have all had City careers, but that was very much their choice. Though Glenn and Neil spent time at Tulletts during the school holidays, I never sought to influence them in what they should go on to do when they finished school.

When he left Whitgift, Glenn chose to join me in the world of finance and began his City career with a banking course at Chemical Bank in 1979. This gave him a thorough insight into the City and he moved to Tullett & Tokyo Forex two years later and stayed with the company until 2004 rising to Head of Cash Equities.

Glenn is fond of telling a tale against himself, about how, before his City career came to end, he was invited to Japan to mark the tenth anniversary of the Tullett tie up with Tokyo Forex. At such a big celebratory do, honoured guests are traditionally invited on stage to acknowledge the audience. To Glenn's dismay, he was first up and when the audience clapped he waved back. On leaving the stage, he saw — to his horror — that all those who followed merely bowed humbly!

Glenn gained his landscape and forestry diplomas at horticultural college in 2005 and now lives with his second wife Karen and their sons Alex and Nicholas in southern Spain where he runs his own landscape gardening business. More recently his company has been involved with geothermal installations in that part of the world.

Neil, meanwhile, insists that, as a child, he didn't know what I did for living, and so therefore was not obviously influenced in his career choice. However, looking back, he feels it was always likely he would follow me into the City. I must admit I had a totally open mind about the subject. Indeed, when Neil said he would be leaving Alleyn's School in Dulwich after doing his O levels, I said: "No you're not."

But Neil had his way and when later he told me he'd had a job offer from rival brokers Harlow's, I said: "If that's the case you'd better come to work for me at Tulletts." Immediately on arrival at Tulletts, Neil was shipped out to Abu Dhani for six months, where he lived in the office flat. He later returned to London for a couple of years before moving on to a posting in Hong Kong. Neil now runs Tullett's exchange operation in New York.

On returning from Iowa University, Jonathan decided to abandon any idea of a sports career. Within a couple of months of arriving home, he got himself a job at Banque Bruxelles Lambert, whose chief dealer Brian Shubrook, and his wife

Pauline, are close friends. Soon after joining BBL, Jonathan found there was little time for athletics any more and played squash, instead. He moved to Danske Bank in Copenhagen in 2002 and resigned in 2006. He is now forging a new career in Monaco in the hedge fund industry.

From a young age, Kevin spent school holidays and each Christmas on the noisy trading floor at Tulletts surrounded by men shouting prices at each other. I imagine he had thoughts of the legal profession as he elected for work experience at the lawyers Peters and Peters, where an old friend, Keith Oliver, is a senior partner.

After school in the UK and his year in Iowa with Jonathan, which brought them very close together, Kevin returned to Britain and his degree at Durham University. While there, he started playing rugby league and at one stage was thinking very seriously about taking it up professionally with Huddersfield Giants. But I advised him otherwise and after he got a 2:1 in Economics and Management, he went on to achieve a masters degree in Business Management and Finance at City University's Cass Business School. After a very tough year, he completed his studies and gained a job at Commerzbank, later moving to Mizuho Capital Markets and on to Deutsche Bank.

Kevin wanted a career where everyone was judged on merit and individual achievement ranked highly. Today, he is involved in corporate sales for Deutsche Bank in London.

At each career stage, Anita and I tried advise him with sound and reasoned arguments. And helping to broadening his experience, Tullett brokers would look after Kevin when they went out for a few drinks around the City!

Not only have the boys had similar interests and careers, but they are also close personally. Even though their work has taken them to different parts of the world, they keep in touch.

And I am pleased to report that my grandchildren are

carrying on the Tullettt sports tradition. Glenn's son Alex is very skilled at go-karting, while Nicholas is a promising rugby player. Neil lives in New York with his second wife, Lynn, and their baby daughter Amy. He has two teenage children — Emily (18) and James (16) — from his first marriage to Sue and they also have the family sporting gene: Emily was a successful tennis and table tennis player at Bede's school in Sussex and is preparing to go to a tennis coaching school, while James was a talented hockey player at Royal Russel school near Croydon.

Kevin met his Danish girlfriend Pia at university and they have been together since. I know it's a source of frustration to them that they get invited to charity events at very short notice. Kevin says it's because I've forgotten how many I've pre-booked the table for and I'm often two short! That's me, I guess. And, anyway, I don't like to let down a charity.

By the time the boys had grown up, Anita felt it was too late for her to return to the broking industry which, since she left, had changed dramatically in the new computer age. And after the boys left home, I think we both realised that the glue which had held things together had finally gone and we were left wondering: "What do we do now?" Anita and I divorced in 2000.

I had known Gloria Saunders for over 20 years before our personal relationship developed. Like me, she has always been keen on keeping fit and we were both members at Bromley Town. Coincidentally, Anita hired Gloria to do some interior decoration for us at Keston.

Gloria, who was born in New Cross, south London, had lived and worked in the Bromley area after her own divorce. Her interior decorating business took off (her first payment was a bottle of wine and a meal out!) as friends recommended her to others and she developed a reputation for excellent work.

We had both been divorced for a while by the time our paths

crossed again at the squash club — after which I invited her to
dinner in November 2000. We saw each other regularly after that
and eventually the relationship reached a point by the summer of
2001 when we decided to live together.

We have a busy social life and attend a number of private and
public functions together. Even so, Gloria finds time to play
racquet ball and is now a keen golfer, while her big project has
been superintending the decoration of our new house near
Cannes, which was completed early in 2006. Her new project is
our Keston home. Gloria has three children — Jane, Darren and
Damon — and we see a good deal of them.

If pressed for a favourite family moment down the years, I
suppose it would have to be the arrival of my first grandchild,
Emily who, as mentioned, was educated at Bede's school in
Sussex.

I have always been neutral in the argument about whether
work can destroy a marriage. While I don't think long hours and
trips abroad enhances a marriage, I neither feel it takes the toll
that many experts and analysts on the subject would have you
believe. I genuinely do not think it contributed greatly to the
breakdown of my two marriages. Inevitably, I suppose, a full
business life does create enforced absence and brings certain
pressures on family time and relationships. I concede that if you
are away for months on end it can create difficulties.

But I don't think such absence puts an unnecessary strain on
domestic life and, indeed, to avoid just that, I tried to involve my
family and they certainly accompanied me on many extended
business trips abroad. I also tried to ensure that I was always with
my family at weekends. And surely it's not simply a matter of the
quantity of time your family gets, but the quality of the time you
give it.

With business still very much to the fore, I have an apartment
in The City, which cuts out unnecessary travelling, when — for

example — staying overnight is convenient for early morning appointments. One of the effects of an excess of travelling in my career is that, these days, I don't want to travel long distances for leisure and general holidays. Gloria and I are perfectly content with the relatively short hop to the villa in the south of France and spend as much time there as we can.

Talking of houses, this leads me, in conclusion, to Keston Park — which is at the heart of my family life. I suppose having witnessed much change one is bound to look for certain forms of continuity. The house at Keston Park has provided continuity for me over the years. I suppose the distinction is this: there are houses and there are homes, some we merely live in and some we come to love. I bought my house in Keston Park in 1971 for £12,500 (funded by my Savage & Heath share sale) and, from the moment I saw it, knew that this would be my home and that I would live in there for a long time, and so it has proved. The swimming pool we had built for the boys, was filled in during the 90s to become a large conservatory.

For all my international travelling and properties owned abroad, it is very much my base — not least because of its location just half an hour or so from the centre of London and being close to important road networks and major airports. Equally, I don't like big houses and this is the perfect size for a family home. Gloria and I are both enthusiastic gardeners and we have a spectacular flower and vegetable garden. Several makeovers later (and one is due in 2007) my home is central to my life over the past 35 years or so and I imagine it always will. In short, nothing will tear me away from it and I intend to remain there!

II

THE INTERESTS

Denis Healey famously observed that the modern politician is merely a career creature lacking any kind of what he calls "hinterland". Most of today's MPs, he insists, are produced by their party apparatus and suffer in terms of both political skills and appeal to the public because they know of no other life than politics.

And, if it's true, that politicians could do their job better if they had wider interests, then the same could be said for decision-making in business. Judgement is a simple cocktail really: a little instinct mixed with a lot of experience. And, the broader your experience, the better your chances of making the right decision. And the better your decisions the better businessman you become.

Although I have been totally committed to my business, I've always believed in an active life outside the office. I've worked hard and played hard and have developed a range of interests that have helped to complement and freshen up my involvement in the world of the money markets and the City generally.

Underpinning all that, however, has been my religious faith. which from an early age has been a central force in my life. At the age of 10 I joined a young persons' social club — a Baptist

Church group called the Covenanters. We were organised into age groups for the sporting and spiritual side of things. In fact, the main reason I joined was to follow a number of my friends who had joined to play soccer and table tennis. A year later though I achieved a scholarship to Whitgift School and, with the pressure of work and school life generally, found the sporting side of the Covenanters, apart from an occasional game of table tennis, faded away. I did, however, continue to attend the Sunday afternoon service.

Over the years I accepted the general tenet of the Baptist faith, and it raised for me a number of unanswered questions. Indeed, while my mind was in turmoil over a number of issues, I was due for National Service. So, with great difficulty, I put these questions to the back of my mind, as I did my time in the army. However, during those days they surfaced regularly and there was little I could do except have faith in my firm belief and compromise with my doubts.

After I was demobilised on my return home, I continued to attend services at the Baptist church with greater maturity — perhaps brought about by being in a war zone for a long period.

My confidence in the faith I have now structured for myself surrounds my strongly accepted tenets at the heart of the Baptist teaching. It has served me well during the past 60 years and I am positive will be with me forever.

One of my biggest interests is politics, which goes back to my childhood. I can trace my core political beliefs to the time I gained a scholarship to Whitgift School and where I enjoyed the intellectual exercise of political argument, so totally unfashionable with the youth of today. Although I got to Whitgift through academic merit, I encountered snobbery among a few of my fellow pupils. My parents were not poor by any stretch of the imagination, but many of the other boys' parents were relatively prosperous. So, the issue of privilege was etched into my consciousness at a relatively early age and so my belief in equal opportunity was born.

Of course, I also came to see that my scholarship arose out of the radical education reforms of the post-war Attlee government which gave me the opportunity to get a foot on life's ladder. It taught me a need to respect those around me and gave me a burning sense that more opportunity should be available to those with ability.

These twin issues of privilege and opportunity have given me a lifelong left-of-centre view of things — some of which are still pretty strong to this day, while others have moderated with time. My views have mostly meant an active support of the Labour Party, although it has not always meant they had my vote at election time. I imagine what some would see as a paradoxical thread running through my politics: at heart, I am left of centre, but my head has occasionally told me to step back from Labour, believing that my interests and those of the country would be better served by others.

Like many in the late 1970s, I had come to view the Labour Party with growing concern: it was in government but not in power, to coin Norman Lamont's celebrated phrase. The economy was in complete disarray: the unions were out of control, there was high taxation and an excess of public spending, funded by borrowing.

The country, quite simply, had not moved with the times. We needed someone tough like Margaret Thatcher with her reforming agenda and, thankfully, she delivered. For that reason I voted Conservative at each general election during the Margaret Thatcher years, while waiting for Labour, so hopelessly bankrupt of ideas and going through what seemed like a collective nervous breakdown, to re-invent itself and show that it was electable and capable of running things once again.

I have never seen any conflict between my business interests and my political beliefs. On the one hand, I firmly believe in capitalism and the role of the marketplace. On the other hand, I believe in compassion, social provision by the state and the need to ensure decent standards for all. This has always put me to the right of the Labour Party and made me a natural supporter of Tony Blair, who, in a way, has taken up the Thatcher legacy with an added compassion and sense of opportunity for all.

My support for Labour over many years took the form of simple membership, attending occasional meetings and helping at election time. During the 80s — and what proved to be the nadir for Labour's fortunes with the years of Michael Foot and Neil Kinnock — I contented myself with the feeling that Mrs Thatcher's strength and reforming zeal was what the country was crying out for. I kept my party membership going in the hope that Labour's time would come again and, of course, it did in the mid-1990s in the shape of Tony Blair.

With the advent of New Labour my backing for the party moved up a gear. I believed wholeheartedly in Tony Blair's programme and his approach to government and was prepared, along with many businessmen, to provide financial support. I joined Labour's 1,000 Club and this brought me into the fold of like-minded people whose involvement and views would be strongly sought in the years that followed. What does my involvement with Labour Party mean in practical terms? It's simply this: membership of the 1,000 Club sees me attending functions, get-togethers at the annual conference and having my views sought from time to time.

By 2003 The Sunday Times was wrongly reporting that my total donations had topped £300,000 and that I was part of the "Champagne Socialist Jet Set" (I think all those who know me will enjoy the incorrect description) organised by Lord Levy, whom it dubbed, somewhat unkindly, "Labour's Mr Cashpoint".

The figures for my donations are a matter of public record, but I never normally comment on them. Circumstances, however, earlier this year put my private backing for Labour even more into the public domain. As I say, I have donated a regular sum to the Labour Party, but in November 2005 I became aware that, as a result of the expense of fighting the previous May's general election, it was in serious debt. Lord Levy spoke to me about the situation and I agreed to lend the party £400,000 at a commercially-agreed rate and the documents were drawn up. The loan was due for repayment in November 2006, but has been extended.

There has been a huge amount of press publicity about Labour's financial backers, almost all of it totally wide of the mark. In the face of much speculation Lord Levy called me in March 2006 to say that Tony Blair had decided Labour should reveal the 12 donors who had lent the party a total of £14m and that my name would be one of them. This did not give me a problem and I instantly agreed.

After the revelation, there was a feeding frenzy of media comment, most of it focusing on Chai Patel, Rod Aldridge and Sir Gulam Noon who, as well as being party backers, were, apparently, on a list of possibles being considered for a peerage. Of course, I cannot speak for my fellow donors about what their motives have been for their financial support of Labour. All I know is this: I have never sought or expected any kind of honour in return for my donations. My CBE was awarded under John Major's Conservative government for services to the financial industry and the driving force behind this came from City institutions.

Obviously, the majority of large donors to the Labour Party are also involved in various charities in terms of financial assistance and the time they give. As a result of which the press have sought to see a connection and worse, some sort of conspiracy, in this.

All I know is that I have given willingly to Labour over many years simply because I have believed in Tony Blair and his reforming zeal and was prepared to back that with money. It has been a great privilege to have been in a position to support Tony Blair, both as party leader and Prime Minister. I think he is immensely talented and I feel he has done a great job, but he would have done an even better one had he been able to take the left of the party with him on his public reform programme. In addition to the often-bitter divisions on Iraq and other aspects of foreign policy, social policy, such as in education and the health service, have brought divisions and, as I write, continue to cloud what is the final year of the Blair era and threatens to rob him of the title of "the great reforming Prime Minister".

Labour's left-wing, both MPs and party activists, seem to be nervous of change, which is a very sad. I think you might argue about the detail of, and maybe the approach to, reform; what you can't argue about, in my opinion, is the need to do so.

What happens when Tony Blair stands down is an intriguing question. It's long been assumed that Gordon Brown will succeed him, and that may well be the case. Even if he does, I don't think the unions and the left of the party can assume that he is necessarily their friend and that they can look forward to the end of New Labour and a return to old-style left-wing policies. I think "the project", as the media likes to refer to it, still has a lot of tread on its tyres.

Into a third term, and on the back of successive election victories, I think what we are seeing, in part, with the current Labour squabbling, is the natural consequence of being in office for so long. Tony Blair is falling foul of it, as did Mrs Thatcher before him. Politicians become a bit jaded, governments run out of steam and electorates get bored. I am, actually, a great believer in the American system of a fixed tenure — two terms of office lasting eight years maximum. That should be long enough for any leader or administration to make their mark. Anything longer than that tends to bring about drift, where there should be energy and ideas. And maybe we could learn from that in Britain.

I also believe that an independent body should provide the strategic thinking for the police, education and National Health Service, thereby providing continuity as political parties change.

I think the whole "loans" episode has raised important questions about the funding of political parties. It's highly unlikely that the public would ever agree to their taxes being used to fund the parties. If it did occur, however, it would remove the union influence in Labour politics. At the same time, the biased press coverage has almost certainly ensured that, in future, individuals will be reluctant to donate or speak to the press. One compromise solution could be for a limit to be placed on the amount parties can receive to finance general elections: with 50% coming from the taxpayer and the rest from individual donations.

A particularly agreeable interest of mine has been with the City liveries. Sir Peter Gadsden, who recently died, introduced me to the Cripplegate Ward Club in the late 70s. My connection with the Worshipful Company of Fruiterers came about directly as a result of my membership, and later master, of the Cripplegate Ward Club. I was then encouraged to join a livery company and, naturally, with my family background, through my father's business with fruit, it made sense that it should be the Worshipful Company of Fruiterers. Today, half of the livery membership comprises those in the fruit trade in the broadest sense— such as growers, pallet makers and canned fruit manufacturers, etc — while half are in professions such as the law, accountancy and banking. This provides a useful variety in the livery's make-up.

We set out to raise money each year through various functions and activities. The livery funds educational courses and donates fruit to various charities around London. Last year was of particular significance being the livery's 400th anniversary and we are trying to secure pledges to the tune of £400,000 — again for educational purposes.

One of the livery's really nice touches is, at the master's choosing, the planting of a tree in the grounds of every organisation we are involved with. At my alma mater, Whitgift School, for example, we planted a mulberry tree, which has pride of place by the school gates. During my year I also had the privilege of planting two trees at Baroness Rothschild's home and winery in Bordeaux.

We are a nomadic livery — the Fruiterers' Hall was burned down in the Great Fire of London — and a very friendly one, full of some splendid people. I've enjoyed my membership very much, particularly my 12 months as Master in 1995-96. There are a number of meetings and dinners to attend each year, the more so for me, being a past Master. I have recently been elected to a new guild — the Guild of International Bankers. The camaraderie within the livery companies and their generous charity donations fits easily into my life.

One thing I am very proud to be involved with, and one which is very close to my heart, is the Olive Tree project. This, in essence, brings together my politics and social concern in a sort of internationalism. The Olive Tree Educational Trust came about through discussions I had with Professor Steve Miller of City University and it was incorporated in October 2003 to promote harmony between communities living in Israel, The West Bank and Gaza.

By studying together for three years at City University it is hoped that Jewish, Palestinian, Druse and Bedouin students will come together through academic and cultural activities, so promoting mutual respect and understanding as well as promoting human rights and fostering economic enterprise. Tuition fees and accommodation costs are met by the Trust.

The idea for Olive Tree arose as a result of a family

connection of Gloria's. The girlfriend of one of her son's was living in Israel and finding it difficult to get to Britain to complete her education and, having spoken to her, I discovered she had liberal views about relations with Palestine, which I found quite encouraging.

Putting these two things together, I thought how useful for the future of the region it would be if students from both countries could travel to Britain and get to know one another. So, I put this idea to Steve who developed it further. We then received a generous financial pledge from Sheikh Mohammed Bin Issa Al Jaber which, along with a donation from myself, helped launch the scheme.

The first batch of 16 students arrived in London in September 2004 (and we now have a further 14) and we like to think that over the three years that the students are together in London tensions between Palestine and Israel would have eased. By the time they return home, you'll have a new generation which has been living and working together and finding, perhaps, a new perspective. When they go back to their countries we expect them to continue their dialogue — possibly via the Olive Tree educational trust past pupils website we are setting up — and this may offer a hopeful sign for that troubled region.

When the students return to Palestine and Israel they are under an obligation to continue the peace-making process by maintaining their links in some kind of cross-border co-operation, hopefully a form of business, which we aim to help them with. We see cross-border businesses as one of the hopes for improved relations in the long-term.

The scheme has got off to a great start, the students have all mixed well over the two years and excelled in their studies. The second batch of students started in the autumn of 2006 when they will overlap for 12 months with the first group who will then be in their final year. And further groups will arrive every few years on a rolling programme.

Olive Tree involves me in a couple of meetings each month, plus other functions. In May 2004, Sheikh Mohammed Bin Issa Al Jaber and myself, who as joint founding patrons of the Olive Tree programme, were priviliged to receive honorary Doctor of Science degrees from City University in a ceremony at The Guildhall.

At the ceremony, I was flattered to hear Steve Miller say of me: "He has shown exactly the same zeal for the promotion of opportunity through education — with an emphasis on initiatives that help young people, particularly those from disadvantaged backgrounds. His philanthropic efforts are extensive — including, for example, his role as a past Chairman of the Lord Mayor's Appeal, his support for City Action and Community Service Volunteers."

Community Service Volunteers (CSV) is, indeed, another great interest of mine. As I've indicated I balance my passionate belief in capitalism and wealth creation with a strong social conscience. As someone who has succeeded in life, I feel I have a responsibility and, indeed, a moral duty, to put something back into society. My thinking has always been: "If you have, you should give."

To that end, CSV is one of a number of causes I have championed. I get asked to become involved with a number of organisations and projects, but what is special about CSV is that it gives practical expression to a lot of my own social beliefs and fits neatly into my politics: that is, people volunteering to do things for other people without any personal gain or reward.

My association began in 2000 following an approach by CSV's Dame Elizabeth Hoodless. I knew about its work and didn't hesitate to answer the call. Over the past few years my role with CSV has grown: I am both chairman of the annual "flagship" event, Make A Difference Day, held in October each year, and of the Awards Committee. Make A Difference Day, efficiently organised by Elizabeth Salter for the last time, brings widespread media publicity for CSV, helping to raise its profile, while introducing fresh members of the public to volunteer their skills for the benefit of others — who are often needy and disadvantaged groups. We normally have in excess of 100,000 volunteers for the "day" — thanks, largely, to Elizabeth.

CSV had a special year in 2005, which was designated The Year Of the Volunteer and there were many events to mark that. My involvement with CSV commits me to a number of meetings throughout the year and I also try to visit as many projects on Make A Difference Day as I can. Given the time, I would like to have a couple of days visiting projects outside London in future.

Education has always been very important to me and I think this has shown in the emphasis I have placed on it with my sons and in my business career. In my own case, and despite my somewhat uncomfortable time at Whitgift soon after the war, I have always been grateful to the school. Whitgift set me on the right road and, with a feeling of gratitude, I have continued to be connected with the school down the years as an old boy and governor.

My continuing association with the school began through the Old Whitgiftians. When I left school I played rugby for the Old Boys and subsequently became a member of the Whitgift School Committee and then chairman, and later President, of The Old Whitgiftian Association. As a result of these activities, I was invited in the late 1990s by the-then headmaster to become a governor of the school and served a full seven-year term. I have occasionally spoken at the school's career evenings and prizegivings.

Staying in touch with the school has allowed me to see the

growth in the school at first hand. Each headmaster has raised the bar in terms of standards, but the contribution of the present head, Dr Christopher Barnett is exceptional and worthy of special mention. His commitment and innovation has seen Whitgift achieve a fine academic record — certainly in the country's top 10 — and in recent years it has started to offer the Baccalaureate as an alternative to A levels. New ideas are being explored, too, with Whitgift establishing connections with schools outside the UK. It has close links with a school in Tokyo, for example. There's no doubt that when the time comes for the excellent Dr Barnett to step down, he will prove a very difficult act to follow.

In addition, the school has a thriving cultural life with all areas of the arts catered for. It has also become a centre of excellence in sport. It has many talented youngsters and tales of the school's sporting achievements are legendary.

The theatre is another great interest of mine and I have my mother to thank for that. Despite the wartime air raids, she dragged me across rubble-strewn streets in London to take refuge — physically and emotionally — in a world, far from the harsh realities of life, being portrayed on the stage. I enjoyed the theatre and took every opportunity to see a play or show. These days many of this country's deprived children get little opportunity to go to the theatre, and, therefore, I was pleased to have the opportunity to do something about it.

About 15 years ago, Judy Vereker, wife of the present Governor of Bermuda, who was its fund-raiser at the time approached Tullett's and I jumped at the prospect of the group sponsoring a pantomime at the Polka Theatre for Children in Wimbledon — choosing it from one of the many applications for support we received, The theatre, which was originally a team of puppeteers, operates in a wonderful building in Wimbledon and Steven Midlaine and his colleagues work unceasingly for young people and this appealed to me. The fact that it co-operates with schools where many of the pupils are from underprivileged backgrounds is vital.

My involvement grew from the initial corporate funding and I joined the committee after a couple of years. More recently I have stepped down to become a patron and I attend as many events as possible and bring along the occasional celebrity. I am totally committed to this particular cause, not least because the alarming fact is, at present, it's only one of two permanent theatre spaces for children in the south of England.

The theatre breaks even on an annual balance sheet of £1.25m and enjoys a 92% seat occupancy for its pantomime season. In fact, a Baptist minister friend of mine Paul Winchester, a former NatWest dealer, enjoys the productions and encourages everybody he meets to take their children to the Polka. For the rest of the year it puts on challenging avant-garde productions which help children see that theatre can offer a message as well as being fun and entertaining.

I suppose sport is one of my original interests, going back to childhood. I have always enjoyed competitive sport, both team games and individual pursuits. At Whitgift I took part in a number of sports — rugby, cricket, cross country, athletics, squash and rifle shooting.

Rugby has been my greatest passion, though, having played at several levels. I turned out for Old Whitgiftians and had something of a "hard man" reputation as an inside centre and outside half. At 18, I was the youngest ever outside half to play for the Old Boys, eventually playing in about 250 games over 12 years. The standard was high enough to get me selected for Surrey in county matches.

I also played rugby in the Army, especially in Malaya. Our battalion side had been reasonably successful until we played the Fijians, the start of Southern Hemisphere rugby. When I arrived in the City with ANZ bank, which had a very good team, I was training two to three times a week and played for Old Whitgiftians on Saturdays and, occasionally, on Sunday for ANZ Bank or United Banks. Although my parents weren't particularly religious, they couldn't bring themselves to watch me on a Sunday as they saw it as a day of rest. "You shouldn't be playing on a Sunday," they said. How times change.

So, the mixture of working in the City and playing rugby was perfect for networking. This was quickly recognised by the partners at Savage & Heath who used to turn up with clients to watch some games. Having played a lot of rugby, I retired from the game at 32 and, remarkable to report, injury-free! In actual fact, I came out of retirement to play half a game against a rival company in which I found myself marking a former British Lions player. It was the usual lively stuff with one colleague commenting on a particularly lively tackle on me: "I can see the imprint of your body in the mud!"

In more recent times I have carried my enjoyment of the game into coaching youngsters, including my sons, in mini rugby at St David's and Greenhayes schools and I have also been a keen follower of the England international side.

I originally played squash at school, but took it up more seriously in 1970 and have played it ever since for fun, fitness and competition. Club squash led to my playing at county level and, in later years, I have taken part in seniors competitions, winning the singles and in 2001 winning the GB Vets Over-65s doubles championship with my partner Ray Rook. This year I am taking part in over-65s and over-70s doubles and over-70s singles.

Motor sport is a great hobby of mine, too. I have always enjoyed cars — the faster the better. I have raced sports cars, Minis, Clubmans, Special GTs and Formula 3, for which you had to pass careful scrutiny within the regulations to qualify and compete as a driver. It was a fun five or six years. My favourite was saloon cars with no quarter given, but at the end of a day's racing we enjoyed each other's company in the bar. I also had a gull-wing Lotus, my first racing car, which I owned and maintained for a season, and I also raced Minis. On one crazy occasion, I remember travelling in a Mini with my eldest son Glenn to the Brands Hatch circuit in Kent. We were towing my racing Mini, and, unbelievably, we were caught speeding going uphill on a road out of Orpington!

Rallying was another passion. In the early 1970s, I took part with Alan Gaunt in the Trans-Sahara and a number of other rallies in a Ford Cortina as a freelance. They lasted three or four weeks and were tough. I lost about 10lbs in each of these events. I eventually stopped my motor sport because it was so time consuming. I settle these days for watching, mainly Formula 1, on television.

One of my earliest hobbies was painting, which broadened somewhat into design during my teenage years at Whitgift. I enjoy oil painting and hope, perhaps vainly, that I will find enough time to paint again, particularly in and around our new home in the south of France. Music, ballet and opera are other interests and I try to get to performances throughout Europe whenever I can. I have attended the opera in Verona annually for the past five years. However, in 2006 we attended the open air opera in the South of France, to make a comparison.

Other interests have been an involvement with the Iron Bridge Trust and I am a former Chairman of the Lord Mayor's Appeal for the West Wing of St Bartholomew's Hospital. I am a Freeman of the City of London and a Friend of the Royal Opera House.

Whether I shall have more time for these interests, or can create more time for even more interests, I cannot say. Having seen my 70th birthday, I think I am happy and thankful to settle for the good health to be able to pursue them at all.

12

THE FUTURE

The end of 2004 was a landmark in my career. That December not only saw my 70th birthday, but also 50 years in the City and the end of my full-time connection with Tullett Liberty. To reflect all this, Gloria and I organised a double celebration in early December at my two "homes from home" — the Chapter One restaurant at Locksbottom, Kent and the London Capital Club off Cannon Street in the City.

I was delighted that so many family, friends and associates — spanning a whole range of interests and involvements over many years — were able to attend those excellent evenings. Principal guests included Lord and Lady Levy (Michael and Gilda), Ken and Eiko Yanagita, who travelled from Japan, Dr Hans Beck and his wife Lena, Dr Christopher Barnett and his wife Laura and William and Valerie Brake. It is not possible to name all who attended that evening, however I would like to make special mention of several old friends: David Straw, David Priest, Chas Stevens, Bruce Collins, Nigel Belle, David Riley, Anthony Fuller and Gordon Freakes.

After the hectic period of partying had passed, I had time to consider over Christmas that "technically" I had retired, yet again. Of course, I had been here before. In 1999 when I was 65, and had stepped back from the frontline running of the business, I was called into action again to help deal with one of the most serious crises the company had ever faced.

Bruce Collins and I pulled the company through and the five years that followed, which allowed me to "dine at the top table" once again, I treated as a real bonus. But, now at 70, it really was time for me to go, re-charge my batteries and re-focus my energies on a whole raft of opportunities that lay before me. My diary was full and there were a lot of things demanding my attention — new business possibilities, giving more time to a range of involvements and the chance to develop fresh interests.

Through those opportunities I hoped to maintain the many friendships and associations I had made in the City and the routines I had become used to over many years — not least, catching the 6.59 train from Orpington! For routines are like old friends, both familiar and comforting, and we often hang on to them as long as we can.

So, what were my feelings as I entered the post-Collins Stewart Tullett era? At this stage in my career I certainly had an overwhelming sense of achievement — how could I fail to have. After all, in thirty-odd years I had built a money brokers from scratch to become the second biggest in the world — this was phenomenal growth in anyone's books. And I think it's true to say that this is what David Riley and I were aiming at when we started out in 1971.

If I was asked what the company's legacy is to the markets, then I would say I believe it will be remembered as a groundbreaker. In so many ways, the company was ahead of its time. But three aspects stand out:

1. Tullett was the first to adopt an approach that saved on the human resource
2. Tullett was the first to put loudspeakers into dealing

rooms – in this way, one person using a microphone
could call, say, ten others using a single keystroke. And
even though this raised questions of transparency and
confidentiality, rivals soon took up the idea and
eventually they were everywhere

3. Tullett's, through a company called Futrend, (and along
with Reuters) were the first to provide prices on screen
which we saved and purchased additional data with a
view to providing current and historic data for the
markets. Reuters were the market leaders in this market.
Sadly, we did not have the management time to develop
Futrend and chose to close the operation

The company also broke new ground by being the first into
New York and the first to consumate a share exchange on the
Tokyo market. New York gave me particular pleasure. It was a
massive breakthrough because, until then, the local brokers'
association was opposed to foreign brokers and, at the same
time, regulations prevented UK clients from dealing with a
broker outside London. It was a fine achievement to break into
this important market.

Overall, though, I'm certain that Tullett's success stemmed
from the way the business was managed. Obviously, the
management was better in some years than others. But despite
such unavoidable unevenness, we, importantly, kept a
management "thread" going through the years, which carried us
forward and kept us on track to maintain targets, make profits
and achieve growth.

As a side issue, such success cannot be achieved without
some cost — and, often it's a personal cost — to the principles
involved. I wouldn't deny the personal price can be very high.
The demands then and now mean your social and family life can
be almost non-existent. For example, in the 1970s and 80s Friday

night was party night in the City. Today, it's Thursdays, which means a decent start to the weekend for most City workers. So, that's progress of sorts — but it's still a tough life with most offices operating from seven-to-seven and, with an evening's entertaining thrown in, that means not arriving home until 10pm.

From all this I think I have learned three main lessons down the years. In terms of man management, it's a simple formula really. I came to see that you have to treat everybody — regardless of who they are, or where they are, in the organisation — the same. I believe we treated others the way we would wish to be treated. Anyone who understands this is half way to becoming a successful manager. By the same token, the moment managers believe they are above it all and become arrogant, management will surely go wrong.

Bruce Collins and I pursued this strategy when we again took over the reins in 1999. And another factor in our drive to pull the company around then was our ability to divorce our business relationship from our out-of-office friendship. While we were close friends we never let that colour our business decisions, which were always based on hard facts, not sentiment or bias.

Finally, there's the vital need in business for sustainability. If a business doesn't have sustainability in whatever form — it may be product development in the short term or overall strategy in the long term — then it invites uncertainty. And uncertainty breeds vulnerability.

It was sustainability that was at the heart of the 1999 crisis that saw my recall to the frontline at Tullett Liberty. As I detailed in an earlier chapter the-then chief executive's decision, without full consultation at board level, to go-ahead with a deal-matching system for securities saw the company haemorrhaging money. Not enough homework had been done and decisions were made without proper costing. With software and marketing eating up money at a rate we could not sustain, we had to discontinue it.

Fortunately, the nature of that market meant that our income was not disturbed too much. There were several companies specialising in on-the-run prices, whereas Tullett's New York dealt in the odd lots and, with fewer staff, still had a similar profit.

Against that background, I considered a number of ventures and possibilities. I took my time throughout 2005 to check out the companies and "kick the tyres" so to speak. As a result, my business interests revolve around three ventures. In two of these — Blue System Inc and Spectron — I am priviliged to be chairman. In the third, Global Betbrokers, I am a non-executive director.

Late in 2005, having reviewed a number of very generous offers, I elected to become Chairman of Blue System Inc, whose Chief Executive Sulim Malook has spent several years in development with a view to fully launching in 2007. Sulim's wife, Jane, is a director and Company Secretary. With their three daughters, they make a charming family.

It's appropriate that Blue System has come to fruition at this time, coinciding as it does with the emergence of the European Union's MiFID (Markets in Financial Instruments Directive) which highlights "best execution" in the markets. MiFID will replace the existing Investment Services Directive, the most significant EU legislation for investment intermediaries and financial markets since 1995. MiFID extends the coverage of the current ISD regime and introduces new and more extensive requirements to which firms will have to adapt, in particular in relation to their conduct of business and internal organisation.

The aim of the ISD was to set out some basic high-level provisions governing the organisational and conduct of business requirements that should apply to firms. It also aimed to harmonise certain conditions governing the operation of regulated markets.

MiFID is a major part of the European Union's Financial Services Action Plan (FSAP), which is designed to create a single market in financial services. It makes significant changes to the regulatory framework to reflect developments in financial services and markets since the ISD was implemented.

Blue System is a revolutionary idea in the financial products markets and my involvement also takes me further along the road of automated deal matching. It is an innovative and advanced provider of market data, analysis and trading solutions to the global financial services industry. Some of the world's largest and most celebrated buy-side and sell-side financial institutions will, hopefully, rely on our technology every day for direct market access, order routing, data dissemination and risk management.

We deliver leading-edge technology and solutions, direct market access and best price excecution at all times. We are in more than 50 exchanges worldwide dealing in equities, futures and options and foreign currencies. We simplify cross-border transactions and ensure that the flows are bi-lateral.

Blue System is regulated which means we are able to provide institutional clearing services through our network of international clearing brokers and dealers.

Perhaps the most striking aspect of our set-up is our pricing structure. We have removed entirely the technology and market data costs inherent within the financial services industry. All our technology is licensed, upgraded, supported and maintained on a no-cost basis, with unencumbered distribution rights. No-cost means no cost to our clients. The cost is only incurred when a transaction is consumated.

Blue System has a specialist software team in London and its full staff line-up is: Mushid Samnani, Young Sun Kim, Darren Chesterton, Alex Korthals Altes and Sikander Merchant. James McCubbin is manager of our Southampton office. We also have two distinguished non-executives; Michael Cole was a senior journalist with the BBC from 1968 to 1988, during which he was best known as its Court Correspondent; he became Director of Public Affairs for Harrods from 1988 to 1998. Bashir Nathoo is the founder and major shareholder in the Splendid Hotels chain and manages and operates more than a dozen London-based hotels. By the beginning of 2007, Blue System was penetrating markets worldwide.

In April 2006, I was asked by Drew Stephens, its CEO, to become chairman of Spectron, one of the world's largest energy brokers, and was appointed a month later. Spectron uses a hybrid voice broking and deal matching system and provides a neutral marketplace for OTC transactions between wholesale clients in, inter alia, natural gas, electricity, crude oil and petroleum products. Spectron's marketplaces allow clients to trade both physical and financially settled energy products.

The group operates one of Europe's largest independent energy marketplace, which clients may access either via a screen-based electronic system or by telephone, and also provides ancillary services such as clearing, indices and data sales. As a neutral intermediary, Spectron takes no proprietary positions.

The Spectron business was established in 1988 and was focused originally on the crude oil market. Following a management "Buy-in/Buy-out" in 1999, the group has developed into a diversified provider of services to the energy trading industry, predominantly in Europe as well as in the USA and Asia. Its clients include many of the world's largest energy producers and marketers, as well as the energy trading departments of large financial institutions.

The group, which has offices in London, Frankfurt, Connecticut, New York, Houston, Washington and Singapore, has enjoyed rapid growth, as energy trading volumes in Spectron's key markets have grown significantly in recent years due to deregulation in the energy industry.

My third involvement is with a UK-based company called Betbrokers, the world's first independent betting brokerage, which aims to be the equivalent of an investment house in betting products. The company as set up by an old friend, Wayne Lochner, who is its CEO. Fellow non-executives in the company are Brian Kaye and Eddie Jordan and a great company secretary Stevie Finninger.

Betbrokers places bets on behalf of clients and operates a hybrid system for spread betting. The client has one account with Betbrokers which, in turn, has accounts with the major bookmakers and betting exchanges. The company's job is to carry out the client instruction as efficiently as possible. Betbrokers operates from a telephone dealing room in Canary Wharf and its brokers are constantly monitoring the market for trading patterns, price moves and any other relevant information that can assist clients

The services are tailored to meet the differing requirements of both punters and bookmakers. For example, some punters don't want to compare prices from across the bookmakers and betting exchanges and then have to spend time managing and funding all those separate accounts. One phone call to Betbrokers' dealing room and they can have access to the entire market. The company has accounts with all the major bookmakers and betting exchanges, thereby enabling clients get a bet at a competitive price. Client funds are held securely in a segregated client account with Barclays Bank.

Betbrokers is about to break even after a short period of operations and in November 2006 the board successfully floated the company on the AIM market.

In both Betbrokers and Spectron there are a large number of former Tullett employees. It is strange to walk through their offices with staff shouting: "Hi, Derek. Good to see you." From my point of view, it's good to see them, too.

Finally, I must mention PPI, a Geneva-based investment company I've been involved with for about six years. The company has been run during this time by Yves Perreard, former chief forex dealer at Union Bank of Switzerland, Danny Schwitzer, retired Senior Manager at UBS Zurich, and Marco Bozzolam, who has left recently to become a director of Credit Suisse in Zurich. These men have not only been business colleagues but have become firm friends and I've greatly looked forward to our quaterly meetings

Although business will continue to dominate my week, (and Gloria will tell you I am busier than ever!), if stepping back a little is to mean anything then I want to take this opportunity of developing my other interests which have become important to me.

Top of the list is the Olive Tree Project, which I hope to take up to a half day a week. This could grow and should see me visiting Israel and Palestine in due course. Then there's the Community Service Volunteers which, with its Make A Difference Day and its 120,000 volunteers in 2005-06, is the largest volunteering charity in the UK. To date, my role has been mainly in support as a patron. But I intend to get more involved and have taken on the responsibility for Make A Difference Day. In 2006 I attempted to commit a whole week to going around the country to visit the various centres taking part in Make A Difference Day. I am patron of The Polka Theatre in Wimbledon and it will always have my support.

I am enjoying supporting my livery companies — the Worshipful Company of Fruiterers and the Guild of International Bankers — many of whose members are close friends. I will also continue to support my old school, Whitgift, and its fine headmaster and his staff, along with the children's theatre in Wimbeldon.

What else is in the diary? Well, I do a lot of daily researching of the markets in general. Although UBS manage the majority of my funds, I am proactive with my adviser William Hiscocks, whose company I also enjoy.

My week, in terms of commitments, is full you might say. But I still find time for other things. Healthwise, I keep as fit as I can, which is increasingly important these days. I play squash regularly up to a reasonably high standard. I also have a gymnasium at home and use the equipment to work off the stresses of everyday life. In addition to which, Gloria and I ski each winter and our new home near Cannes can offer us sunshine, fine food and wine. Fortunately, only ten minutes away is an excellent squash club, owned by my old friends, Clive and Debbie Stokes, and boasting excellent squash professionals.

As you can see, "retirement" does not really apply here. However old I am, wherever I am, I will always be busy. I keep active, energetic and mentally alert and this allows me to give something back to society. Clearly, I haven't seen the last of the 6.59 from Orpington, after all.